pocketbooks

01 Green Waters

02 Atoms of Delight

03 Love for Love

04 Without Day

05 Wish I Was Here

06 Wild Life

07 Grip

08 Distance & Proximity

09 The Way to Cold Mountain

10 The Order of Things

11 Mackerel & Creamola

12 The Libraries of Thought & Imagination

13 Unravelling the Ripple

14 Justified Sinners

15 Football Haiku

Frontispiece: 'Nonsense methodised' by Allan Ramsay (1684–1758) and Couper the painter. Reproduced by kind permission of Sir John Clerk of Penicuik.

The Order of Things

Scottish sound, pattern and concrete poetry

The Order of Things

Edited by Ken Cockburn
with Alec Finlay

pocketbooks
Morning Star Publications
Polygon

2001

Published by:
pocketbooks
Canongate Venture (5), New Street, Edinburgh, EH8 8BH.

Morning Star Publications
Canongate Venture (5), New Street, Edinburgh, EH8 8BH.

Polygon
22 George Square, Edinburgh, EH8 9LF.

Designed by Lucy Richards with Alec Finlay.
Typesetting and artworking by Colin Sackett.
Additional typesetting by Cluny Sheeler.
Printed and bound by The Bath Press, Bath.

Published with the assistance of grants from the Scottish Arts Council National
Lottery Fund and the Highlands and Islands Enterprise (HI Arts).

A CIP record is available from the British Library.

ISBN 0 7486 6290 1

List of Contents

11   Editor's Acknowledgements

13   Introduction
      Ken Cockburn & Alec Finlay

23   Sound Poem Kit

37   Abecedarian

53   A Poem Containing

87   Secrets Seen

101   Black Block

113   The Order of Things

125   Two Gardens

135   Acrobats

145   Blue Happening Theatre

161   Macaroni

173   A Horse's Meal

177   Commentaries

191   Notes

197   Bibliography

199   Index of Authors

200   Acknowledgements

      Aeolus CD 'The Order of Things'

Dedicated to the memory of Alan Woods (1956–2000)

Editor's Acknowledgements

This project was conceived and initiated by Alec Finlay, whom I would like to thank for the invitation to take on the role of co-editor. Many of the poems and much of the background material were sourced by him, and I am grateful for his support and suggestions throughout the editing process. My thanks, for their patience, go to everyone who submitted material. Thanks also to Kirsten Lass and Jessie Sheeler for their annotations of Douglas Young's Greek; Professor Ronny Jack and Dr James Reid-Baxter for their advice on Renaissance pattern poems; to Ronald Stevenson for his guidance as to our use of the excerpt from his *Passacaglia on DSCH*; to Hamish Whyte for providing uncollected material by Edwin Morgan; to Stuart Mills for providing material by Ian Hamilton Finlay; and to Colin Sackett for accepting the challenge of typesetting such a visually diverse body of work. The copyright holders are referred to in the 'Acknowledgements', but I would like to extend my thanks to all the individuals who have suggested and made available material for inclusion. Many poems, especially those previously unpublished in book form, were sourced through the Scottish Poetry Library's INSPIRE catalogue. I would also like to thank Alison Bowden at Polygon; Zöe Irvine, who produced the audio CD; and Robin Gillanders, Werner J. Hannapel, Pia Simig and Ian Hamilton Finlay who provided the photographs. Finally, I would like to record my appreciation of the support offered by the staff of pocketbooks: Laura Coxson, Sophy Dale, Alison Humphry and Cluny Sheeler.

Ken Cockburn

Words and Things

There have always been two sorts of poetry which are, for me at least, the most 'poetic'; they are firstly, the sort of poetry which seems to be music just forcing itself into articulate speech, and secondly, that sort of poetry which seems as if sculpture or painting were just forced or forcing itself into words.[1]

Ezra Pound

This anthology takes as its starting point the small but influential body of concrete poetry produced in Scotland in the 1960s, and includes examples of contemporary poems which emerged from that period of experiment. If it had stopped there it would have been a survey of experimental poetry in a small northerly European nation. Our editorial approach, however, aimed to open the anthology further by including older poetic forms, many of which have been continued, revived or developed in the twentieth century. The Concrete Poetry movement is a late episode in Modernism which, when presented alongside its precursors, suggests alternative routes through the landscape of Scottish poetry as a whole. Arranging the contents of the anthology according to form rather than chronology offers surprising and often illuminating points of contact between poems, writers and eras. The anthology demonstrates the vital creative energy that comes from the interplay of tradition and experiment – a defining feature of Scottish culture.

With concrete poetry, Scotland connected to an international avant-garde movement in a manner barely conceivable today. Indeed, the very notion of an avant-garde has been undermined by the commodification of art. While contemporary visual artists have continued to subvert dominant modes of representation, poetry has on the whole retained conventional literary discourse as the norm, and reaps the consequences: compare the shortlist for the Forward Prize with that for the Turner Prize, and the level of public debate around each.

In Scotland, political devolution was preceded by de facto cultural devolution, and in the 1980s and '90s prose-writers redefined Scotland and its place in the world. Poetry played its part, and much fine work has been written over the past two decades by older writers like Iain Crichton Smith as well as a new generation led by John Burnside, Robert Crawford, Kathleen Jamie and Don Paterson. These younger poets have largely held to conventional poetic forms. This is in itself no bad thing: as Pound wrote of Yeats, 'there is no need for a poet to repair each morning of his life to the Piazza dei Signori to turn a new sort of somersault'.[2] Nonetheless, this anthology highlights a period of experimentation, and raises the question as to why it should have been so overlooked during the past two decades.

Five hundred years since the advent of print technology, written language, in a form 'standardised' by print, is afforded an authority denied spoken language – a fact acknowledged by the English word for a person who writes: author. (Compare the very different connotations of 'bard', 'troubadour' or 'minstrel'.) While poetry's technical features continue to be based in spoken language – metre, rhyme, alliteration, assonance, etc. – most contemporary poems are read rather than heard. Modes of spoken language, meanwhile, are increasingly judged against their proximity to written language. On the one hand, print has afforded the poet the opportunity to use structures outwith spoken language, while on the other, it has asserted a 'standard' written language which limits poetry's engagement with speech (an engagement that is complicated or enriched in Scotland by the co-existence of Gaelic, Scots and English).

Concrete poetry derived much energy from the meeting of innovation and tradition, exploring the visual and phonic possibilities of language beyond 'standard' printed or spoken forms: Edwin Morgan presenting Nessie, that most Scottish of clichés, in a sound poem; Ian Hamilton Finlay creating a poetic 'net' using found fishing-boat names. Morgan's monster is a radical extension of Pound's 'articulate speech'. Finlay's 'Sea Poppy 2', which predates the poem-objects and inscriptions he went on to create at Little Sparta, extends Pound's sense of the inscribed word. While taking their lead from Modernism, these poems also recall the oral traditions and inscriptions of the ancient world.

* * *

John Purser, in *Scotland's Music*, locates the origins of music in the natural world: '*ceol* is the Gaelic word for music, but it does not mean the same thing, as it has nothing whatever to do with Greek muses. *Ceol* means a sound like the sound the birds make'.[3] There are examples of Gaelic poetry which attempt an equivalent of birdsong (Purser speculates that this was originally a means of entrapment). These poems imitate in language something essentially non-verbal, by means of sound and rhythm rather than by the explicit meaning of the words. Such 'early music' informed later musical developments including *canntaireachd*, a sung method of recording bagpipe music. Included here are two contemporary variations composed by the artist Kevin Henderson, himself a piper.

While sound poems are related to music, they tend to subvert conventional expectations of the 'content' of the voice by promoting 'abstract' sound above semantic content, and rhythm above melody. Being both imitative of the sounds of the external world (now those of technology as much as of nature), and realised physically by the body, sound poetry has been described as 'open-ended, improvisational, temporal rather than spatial in its organisation; it moves into the flux and uncertainty of language set free'.[4] These characteristics contrast with much of the other poetry in this anthology, which has been conceived in terms of written language. Just as sound poetry begins beyond the 'content' of spoken language, so these other poems begin beyond the 'content' of written language, in their use of visual, sequential or other organising elements.

Individual letters as they have come down to us have certain associations. In Gaelic, each letter is linked to a tree as a mnemonic, while in English the Greek letters 'alpha' and 'omega' have become synonyms for 'beginning' and 'end'. In 'Alpha' Edwin Morgan uses the alphabet to represent a god-like figure, a device perhaps borrowed from St Columba's hymn, 'Altus Prosator',[5] in which each stanza begins with a consecutive letter of the alphabet. The poem is here an article of faith suggesting a creation myth of language, in which 'scripture' is seen as superior to common discourse.

The 'hidden' meaning of an acrostic – most commonly a name, whether religious, dedicatory or amorous – remains obscure without a written version of the text. This recalls the widespread belief in 'secret' or sacred names. The amatory acrostic similarly holds a magical charge. This literary aspect also crosses over into music, where a composer such as Ronald Stevenson can derive a musical theme from a sequence of letters, D S C H or B A C H. In the case of a composer like Shostakovich, working under the shadow of Stalin, such coded messages grew out of a need for secrecy.

The naming of places is one of the most essential linguistic acts. In Scotland, given the historical mix and flow of languages, the meaning of many place-names is now obscure or corrupt. This can lead to a greater suggestiveness as to the 'meaning' of place-names, already rich with associations. To make a poem comprising only of place-names evokes both a physical landscape and ways of seeing it: the poet's view derived from the names chosen, and the collective and historical meanings accumulated by the names themselves. While city street names often bear no literal relationship to place, there are purely local names, such as those given to stretches of the River Teviot in John Murray's 'Pool Poem', that specifically connect with their environment. Ian Hamilton Finlay's use of fishing-boat names reminds us of the poetry inhering in folk traditions, while the names themselves act as invocations or blessings for vessels that are subject to the unpredictable forces of the sea. Arranged in a circle the poet creates a free-floating metaphor, suggesting the round cast net, the circle of the horizon, human endeavours, and the ongoing life cycle.

Finlay's poems recall the earliest of list poems, the 'Catalogue of the Ships' in Book II of *The Iliad*. Lists and catalogues evince the power the act of naming has to recollect and evoke things, in their specificity, not as metaphor but as the reconstitution of the absent. In discussing MacDiarmid's 'poetry of fact', Roderick Watson writes that 'the fact is used rather like the found object in art, its context is changed, but itself must remain intrinsically unchanged except through association with its context; any otherwise and it loses its identity'.[6]

Perhaps the only true originality is that of form. Certainly this has been a major concern of twentieth-century poetry. William Carlos Williams wrote:

> it isn't what [the poet] says that counts as a work of art, it's what he makes, with such intensity of perception that it lives with an intrinsic movement of its own to verify its authenticity. Your attention is drawn every now and then to some beautiful line or sonnet-sequence because of what is said there. So be it. To me all sonnets say the same thing of no importance ... there is no poetry of invention without formal invention, for it is in the intimate form that works of art achieve their exact meaning.[7]

One type of formally innovative poetry is that which uses visual devices. Such 'pattern poetry' goes back at least to ancient Greece, and examples can be found, albeit fragmentarily, in most European literatures up to the nineteenth century, by the end of which, however, 'pattern poetry had slipped into great obscurity and the new wave of visual poetry was just beginning'.[8] This decline may be explained by the ascendancy of rationalism, and the waning of religious belief, which starved these word-images of their 'magical' charge. The British tradition of pattern poems is slight, and there are few examples from Scotland. Most pattern poems are mimetic, and it is perhaps the most limited of visual forms used in poetry. An inventive example is Drummond's pyramid-shaped poem created by lines of progressively longer length, mostly couplets with end-rhymes which help the whole cohere. As a modern example, Morgan's 'Pomander', as well as using the object's visual shape, also restricts itself to the sounds of its source-word, thus relating everything it contains to its (linguistic and literal) container.

Concrete poetry in its 'classic phase' (internationally circa 1955 to 1968, and in Scotland from about 1962) extended the possibilities of visual poetry by developing such Modernist qualities as 'self-reflexiveness, juxtaposition and simultanism',[9] and by moving away from mimetic forms to embrace the new visual universe of electronic technologies. Its precursors are to be traced in the visual arts as much as in literature, particularly in Futurism, Cubism and Constructivism. In literature Pound is a key figure. His work created a deep and dense allusiveness in the 'expansive' form of *The Cantos*: 'allusion not as ornament but as precise means of making available total energy of any previous situation or culture'.[10] His aim was to establish connections which, if rendered explicitly, would fail to achieve the charge of epiphany, the momentary, Zen-like illumination when such connections are grasped intuitively rather than intellectually through the unfolding of a coherent linear narrative.

Concrete poetry uses similar devices, but it operates within a deliberately more restricted field, focusing on a limited number of words, and on syntactic innovation, or by presenting the poem spatially and typographically. It also aspired to existence 'in the world', as Edwin Morgan outlined: 'the concrete poem isn't meant to be something you would come across as you turned the pages of a book. (Most concrete poems, still are, but that is not the ideal.) It would rather be an object that you passed every day on your way to work, to school or factory or office: it would be in life, in space, concretely there'.[11] Morgan, and Ian Hamilton Finlay, were the main practitioners of concrete poetry in Scotland. Morgan's work in this field (which includes translations from the Brazilian *Noigandres* poets and German-language poets such as Eugen Gomringer and Ernst Jandl) is one aspect of a fertile and varied, yet resolutely literary œuvre. Finlay – who still refers to himself as a poet – has extended his literary activity in various ways: as a publisher; as a maker, of toy-boats among other things; and as a composer of neoclassical gardens. His ability to create poem-objects, inscriptions and sculpture is the prime example of the possibilities concrete poetry represented.

Gomringer, one of the pioneers of concrete poetry, referred to his poems as 'constellations' – poems where the relations between the individual elements are fixed, and the field of the poem is perceived as individual elements and a whole. These visual, as opposed to a lineal, texts later gave way as Gomringer reintroduced permutation, repetition, and inversion. In 'emergent poems' secondary lines are 'extracted' from the content of the first. As with concrete poetry, a limited range of materials is manipulated to maximum effect, a kind of poetic 'splitting of the atom', which releases energy or meaning in all directions, from a single, unified source.

Just as an art work can exist conceptually, as an idea rather than as an object, so too there are poems which exist as hypotheses or paradoxes for the reader to consider or respond to. Gerry Loose's variations on the *I Ching* suggest how ancient this tradition is. Such poems connect with the rhymes used by children as open structures for play. Some children's poems echo aspects of sound poetry, with their made-up words enjoyed for rhythmic and tonal effects. These poems entertain and teach; give pleasure to both the ear and the mind; and are learned and used without the mediation of any 'authority'.

As for poetry in the age of the PC and the Internet, it seems that computers have influenced the presentation and publication of poetry rather than creating new poetic forms. Instant self-publication on the world wide web is now a reality, but most poems published on websites or discussed in newsgroups would fit easily into more traditional modes of publishing. The computer does, however, enable the non-linear presentation of a text, not possible in a book. Peter McCarey's *Syllabary*, for example, a large-scale work in progress, offers an infinite number of connections between the individual poems that make up the work as a whole. The poet in no way abdicates responsibility for the creation of the work, but allows the reader greater flexibility in their reading, extending the syntactical innovations that the concrete poets discovered, and allowing the work to resonate in ways beyond the poet's control.

* * *

Rumours of the demise of the book have been greatly exaggerated. The traditional linear text has also retained its dominant position. But visual, pattern, concrete and sound poetry, and the new possibilities of sequence offered by the computer, reflect the ways in which the act and experience of reading are still evolving. As we move into the twenty-first century, global capitalism and its handmaidens, electronic technology and 'standard' English, have created an increasingly homogenised world. The long-term outlook is unpredictable, but to make any sense of their time poets must both come to terms with evolving technology and retain or create a necessary critical distance from it, reapplying or inventing the necessary means to do so.

Ken Cockburn
Alec Finlay

1   From 'The Later Yeats' in *Literary Essays of Ezra Pound* (Faber & Faber, London), 1954

2   ibid. p.378

3   John Purser: *Scotland's Music* (BBC/Mainstream), 1992

4   Stephen Scobie: 'Signs of the Times: Concrete Poetry in Retrospect', in *Cencrastus*, no. 22, 1986

5   'The Maker on High', which Morgan himself has translated.

6   Roderick Watson: 'Hugh MacDiarmid and the Poetry of Fact', in *Stand* vol. 9 no. 4, 1968, p.28

7   William Carlos William: 'Author's Introduction to *The Wedge* (1944)', in Selected Essays (New Directions, New York), 1969, p.257

8   Dick Higgins: *Pattern Poetry, Guide to an Unknown Literature* (University of New York Press), 1987

9   Stephen Scobie, op. cit., p. 24

10 Ezra Pound: letter to Marshall McLuhan, 12 June 1951 (Canada's National Public Archives, Ottawa)

11 Edwin Morgan: 'Concrete Poetry' in *Peace News*, 20 August 1965

Sound Poem Kit

Sound Poems
Bird Song

· in the beginning was the word ·
in thi beginning was thi wurd
in thi beginnin was thi wurd
in thi biginnin was thi wurd
in thi biginnin wuz thi wurd
n thi biginnin wuz thi wurd
nthi biginnin wuzthi wurd
nthibiginnin wuzthiwurd
nthibiginninwuzthiwurd
· in the beginning was the sound ·

Tom Leonard

from Guthan nan Eun
Voices of Birds

A' Chearc   The Hen
Tog, tog, tog, tog,
Tog an rud a dh'fhàg mi,
Ge beag an t-ugh, ge beag an t-ugh,
Tha stà ann, tha stà ann.

An Trilleachan ('s i toirt caismeachd do'n isean)   The Oystercatcher
Eòin bhig, eòin bhig,
Bi glic, bi glic;
Fo dhìon, fo dhìon,
Fo dhìon, fo dhìon.

Oran na h-Eala   Song of the Swan
Gu-bhi-gì, gu-bhi-gò,
Gu-bhi-gì, gu-bhi-gò,
Gu-bhi-gì, gu-bhi-gò,
Gu-bhi-gì, gu-bhi-gò,

Mo chasan dubh,
Mo chasan dubh,
Mo chasan dubh,
'S mi fhìn glégheal.

Chreachadh mo nead,
Chreachadh mo nead,
Chreachadh mo nead,
'S mi fhìn an Eirinn.

Traditional Gaelic

Ceileireadh (Earrann)
Twittering (Fragment)

Fa liu o ho ao ri o ho ao o ho
Svirrr-r-r *rrererere* drrit kokokoko
Air farail ail ò hao ri uh-POOMBH rì hò hill eò
KolloRAP-kolloRAP gah-HONK bheep-bhibew
TrruEEH-e **ririririririri** prreeepkeeh air fà lì leò
Piuu kraah-ap zraaaach trrrt whee-whee-**whew**
AArroo pjak pfEEoo tseeizLITT hù gò ho rò leathag
Whedde-wehk krsch chu-chu-cho hò hi iù a
OO-ooe OO-ooe OO-ooe **be-beeezh** kyang-**ung**-ung
E ho ì ùrabh ò rò ho chiù prrak trruEEh-e kluit *gullagullagulla*
Pseeee hjuuk kje-kjah libh ò hò ri ghealladh
DruOO-u jijijijijijiji pfEEoo ho ì ò ho nà libh i
O hi a hao schaahr kruuht ktchay *poopoopoopoo* chuEESH
Chu WIK thcair kIEEu kloowee-kow-klawi
Hiu na tsip hao ri o hoireann **tixixixixix** o ro ho èile
Pyittittittittitt-ett-ett CHEkorekuVEH e ho hi ri ri o hò gu
REEHew kiERR-ik dirrrrp *quiquiquiqui* psEE-ep seeuuee
Piip-piip-piirr rerrrp-rerrrp charadee-deeoo **pEEE-lu**

Rody Gorman

        tra ra ra ramo
         tra ra ra ramo
              ramon ramon
                        montane montane
                        tramont tramonte tramonte ontane
            onta tan onta
             onta tan onta
                rama tan rama
                   tan tan tan
                              tram
                   tan tan tan
                                  tram
                   tramo tramonte
            tramo tramonte
          tantra mon tantra
    tantra mon tantra
          tramont tramont
                    montane montane
          ram
                tra
                   amo mont amo
                    tantramo tan
                    tantramo tan

t   r   a   m   o   n   t   a   n   e

Dilys Rose

Coire Fhionn Lochan

lapping of the little waves
breaking of the little waves
spreading of the little waves
idling of the little waves

rippling of the little waves
settling of the little waves
meeting of the little waves
swelling of the little waves

trembling of the little waves
dancing of the little waves
pausing of the little waves
slanting of the little waves

tossing of the little waves
scribbling of the little waves
lilting of the little waves
sparkling of the little waves

leaping of the little waves
drifting of the little waves
running of the little waves
splashing of the little waves

Thomas A. Clark

On a Lone Shore

Sea – Boomflapswirlishoo.
　Boomflapswirlishoo.

Bird – Weewee. Weewee.

Sea – Boomflapswirlishoo.
　Swirlishoo. Swirlishoo.

Bird – Weewee. Weewee.

　'An' the sky looks on
　Wi' a'e muckle white e'e.
　It's the tither, I'm thinkin',
　I'll be ha'in on me.'

Hugh MacDiarmid (1892–1978)

The Loch Ness Monster's Song

Sssnnnwhuffffll?
Hnwhuffl hhnnwfl hnfl hfl?
Gdroblboblhobngbl gbl gl g g g g glbgl.
Drublhaflablhaflubhafgabhaflhafl fl fl –
gm grawwwww grf grawf awfgm graw gm.
Hovoplodok-doplodovok-plovodokot-doplodokosh?
Splgraw fok fok splgrafhatchgabrlgabrl fok splfok!
Zgra kra gka fok!
Grof grawff gahf?
Gombl mbl bl –
blm plm,
blm plm,
blm plm,
blp.

Edwin Morgan

hiharara hiharara

hhedari hiharara hioemto hinem

heenI hheendi haemda haemda hheendi haemda hioemto hinemto

hioemto hinemto hheende hheende hheendi heenI hheende hheende hhedari

hinemto hinem hherede hherede hhedari hedili hherede hherede hedili

hioemto hinemto haenda haenda hiendi heenI haenda haenda

hioemto hinemto hiharara hiharara hhedari hedili hadre hiharara

hioemto hinemto haenda haenda hiendi heenI haenda haenda

hioemto hinem hiharara hiharara hhedari hedili hiharara

hioemto hinem hiharara hiharara hhedari hedili hiharara

hioemto hinemto haenda haenda hiendi heenI haenda haenda

hioemto hinemto hiharara hiharara hhedari hedili hadre hiharara

hioemto hinemto haenda haenda hiendi heenI haenda haenda

hinemto hinem hherede hherede hhedari hedili hherede hherede hedili

hioemto hinemto hheende hheende hheendi heenI hheende hheende hhedari

heenI hheendi haemda haemda hheendi haemda hioemto hinemto

hhedari hiharara hioemto hinem

hiharara hiharara

hiharara hiharara

hiharara hiharara hiharara hiharara

hiharara hiharara hiharara hiharara hiharara hiharara hiharara

hiharara hiharara hiharara hiharara hiharara hiharara hiharara hiharara hiharara

hiharara hiharara hiharara hiharara hiharara hiharara hiharara hiharara

hiharara hiharara hiharara hiharara hiharara hiharara hiharara hiharara

hiharara hiharara hiharara hiharara hiharara hiharara hiharara hiharara

hiharara hiharara hiharara hiharara hiharara hiharara hiharara

hiharara hiharara hiharara hiharara hiharara hiharara hiharara

hiharara hiharara hiharara hiharara hiharara hiharara hiharara hiharara

hiharara hiharara hiharara hiharara hiharara hiharara hiharara hiharara

hiharara hiharara hiharara hiharara hiharara hiharara hiharara hiharara

hiharara hiharara hiharara hiharara hiharara hiharara hiharara hiharara hiharara

hiharara hiharara hiharara hiharara hiharara hiharara hiharara hiharara hiharara

hiharara hiharara hiharara hiharara hiharara hiharara hiharara

hiharara hiharara hiharara hiharara

hiharara hiharara

Kevin Henderson

Sound Poem Kit

Tamiya
Riko
Peco
Pyro
Trix
Hasegawa
Revell
Bandai
Fujimi
Veron
Wrenn
Frog
Aurora

Ian Hamilton Finlay

Unscrambling the Waves at Goonhilly

telfish
dogstar
sarphin
doldine
telwhal
narstar
sardock
haddine
dogwhal
narfish
doldock
hadphin
dogdock
hadfish
dolwhal
narphin
hadwhal
nardock
teldock
hadstar
sarwhal
nardine
dogphin
dolfish
sarfish
dogdine
dolstar
telphin
sarstar
teldine
sardine
dolphin
haddock
narwhal
dogfish
telstar

Edwin Morgan

Mavie Sang

tillieloot tillieloot tillieloot

Mavie – Scots for the songthrush
Valerie Gillies

Abecedarian

Alchemies
Alphabets
Acrostics

Arcady

A B C D E F G H I J K L M N O P Q R S T U V W X Y Z

Some Questions on the Poem

1. The poem is no more than an alphabet with a title. Why should an alphabet be presented as a poem and given the title 'Arcady'?

2. 'Roam' is a verb we associate with Arcady. Can one roam among the letters of the alphabet? Might it be that the letters are compared to the fields and forests, mosses and springs of an ancient pastoral landscape? If so, why?

3. Is it relevant to the effect of the poem that the letters are given caps, when they might be in lower case? Could letters possibly have existed before words? Can you imagine their appearance?

4. The original Dada-ists of 1916 wrote a number of poems composed entirely of single letters. Do you think that 'Arcady' is, (a) a non-poem; (b) a neo-Dada poem; (c) a poem that tries to civilise a neo-Dada cliché by turning it into a light-hearted classical conceit?

A Question on the Questions

In your opinion do the questions show a classical conceit?

Ian Hamilton Finlay

On the Invention of Letters

Tell me what genius did the art invent,
The living image of the voice to paint;
Who first the secret how to colour sound,
And to give shape to reason, wisely found;
With bodies how to clothe ideas taught,
And how to draw the picture of a thought:
Who taught the hand to speak, the eye to hear
A silent language roving far and near;
Whose softest noise outstrips loud thunder's sound,
And spreads her accents through the world's vast round:
A voice heard by the deaf, spoke by the dumb,
Whose echo reaches long – long time to come:
Which dead men speak, as well as those alive –
Tell me what genius did this art contrive.

The Answer

The noble art to Cadmus owes its rise,
Of painting words, and speaking to the eyes;
He first in wondrous magic fetters bound
The airy voice, and stopp'd the flying sound.
The various figures, by his pencil wrought,
Gave colour, form, and body to the thought.

Anon (1833)

Vools

A black, E white, I reid, U green, O blae: vools,
Ae day Ah'll tell o your orra comin:
A, jet, vellous vest o plosive flies bummin
Aroun the fell, sair stenches o aidle-pools,

Pits o mirk; E, frankness o yoams an o tents,
Prood glacier-launces, white kings, chitterin umblie;
I, purpies, spat bluid, lauchter on lips comelie
In ragin tene or bedruckenness o repents;

U, tydes, divine thrummin o viridian seas,
Peace o girsin-launds skailit wi kine, peace that drees
Lines alchemie prents on braid broos that panse an grien;

O, owerhailin Trumpet's ferlie rowth o brayin,
Silences bi Warlds an bi Angels owergane:
– Oh, Omega, the violet beam o Her Een!

Orra – strange
vellous – velvety
vest – jacket
aidle-pools – middens
yoams – vapours
umblie – white umbelifer,
e.g. queen anne's lace
tene – anger
bedruckenness – intoxication

girsin-launds – pastures
skailit – dotted
drees – entails
panse – think
grien – yearn
ferlie – strange
rowth – abundance

Tony McManus, after Arthur Rimbaud (1854–91)

The Apple Peel Alphabet

A can band her eyes with black
B can not divide
C can test the strength of love
D can never hide
E has three within her head
F has faithful two
G has crossed her tongue with lies
H is always true
J can beckon all before her
K can point to love and hate
L can set her right again
M can only stand and wait
N goes up and won't come down
O is blind to such good grace
P is always buxom P
Q will pull a yahoo face
R can walk in wanderlust
S can slip in slime
T can see no sight of stars
U can reach in time
V has stretched in supplication
W will win
Y has opened up her heart
and Z will sin, will sin

now X alone can come to trust
 and love
 without the quiz
 that takes away the mystery
 and tells her
who *I* is.

Pete Morgan

Alpha

A is for atlas, but I am not in it.

B is for beehive, but I have the honey.

C is for cheesecloth, but I shall not materialize.

D is for Darwin, but I am a mutation.

E is for ecstasy, beyond your apprehension.

F is for fools – how are you, my friends?

G is for gunfire, all in the day's work.

H is for high altitudes – for some.

I is for invisibility – see?

J is for jailer, but mine is not born yet.

K is for knell, but mine is not tolled yet.

L is for law, but I have none.

M is for mantra, but mine is silent.

N is for nature, but I am beyond it.

O is for owls, but wisdom is for me.

P is for plot, and that you have not got.

Q is for quick, and you had better be.

R is for rust on your trap – look!

S is for sweetness I stole from the stars.

T is for truth, terrible as fire.

U is for untruth, an old yellow tooth.

V is for veil, and mine is of iron.

W is for war, but I do not advise it.

X is for xerox, but I have no copy.

Y is for you as you sink in the grave.

Z is for zero, and that's all your secret.

Edwin Morgan

A Colomne of 18 lynes seruing for a Preface
to the Tragedie ensuying.

1   E i f   1
2 E c h o 2
3 help that both 3
4 t o g e t h e r   w e , 4
5 Since cause there be, may 5
6 now lament with tearis, My 6
7 murnefull yearis. Ye furies als 7
8 with him, Euen Pluto grim, who dwells 8
9 in dark, that he, Since chief we se him 9
10 to you all that bearis The style men fearis of 10
11 Dirae, I request, Eche greizlie ghest that dwells 11
12 beneth the see, With all yon thre, whose hairs ar snaiks 12
12 full blew, And all your crew, assist me in thir twa: 12
11 Repeit and sha my Tragedie full neir, The 11
10 chance fell heir. Then secundlie is best, Deuills 10
9 void of rest, ye moue all that it reid, 9
8 With me in deid lyke dolour them 8
7 to griv', I then will liv' in 7
6 lesser grief therebi. Kyth 6
5 heir and try your force 5
4 ay bent and quick, 4
3 E x c e l l   i n 3
2 s i k   l i k e 2
1   i l l ,   1
a n d   m u r n e   w i t h
me. From Delphos syne
Apollo cum with speid: Whose
shining light my cairs will dim in deid.

E	if Echo help, that both together w	E
(S	ince cause there be) may now lament with teari	S
M	y murnefull yearis. Ye furies als with hi	M
E	uen Pluto grim, who dwells in dark, that h	E
S	ince chief we se him to you all that beari	S
T	he style men fearis of Dirae: I reques	T
E	che greizlie ghest, that dwells beneth the S	E
W	ith all yon thre, whose hairis ar snaiks full ble	W
A	nd all your crew, assist me in thir tw	A
R	epeit and sha my Tragedie full nei	R
T	he chance fell heir. Then secoundlie is bes	T
D	euill void of rest, ye moue all that it rei	D
W	ith me, indeid, lyke dolour thame to gri	W
I	then will liv', in lesser grief therebi	I
K	ythe heir and trie, your force ay bent and quic	K
E	xcell in sik lyke ill, and murne with m	E

> From Delphos syne Apollo cum with speid,
> Whose shining light my cairs wil dim in deid.

James VI (1566–1625)

Hugh MacDiarmid

Hou sall a makar makarize your name,
Uisdein MhicDhiarmaid, Christopher Murray Grieve?
Greatest o Makars, as the young believe,
Heraud o Scotland's swith renascent fame,
Megaphone that dunnered wide wi clangorous grame
Aa ower the realm wi raucle words to deave
Complacent cuifs and gar half-deid Scots live,
Drastic assertor o our nation's claim,
Isna it time ye practised what ye preach,
Archipoeta plasticissime?
Renew your neo Lallan organ-peals,
Μακάρων τὸ πρὶν δὴ τρισμακάρτατε
Iconoclast even o your ain ideals,
Dinna get drouned amang your wrecks o speech!

Douglas Young (1913–1973)

Stella Cartwright
(for her birthday – 15 May 1982)

So, once in the 50s
There was this crazy chap, high among clouds,
Edinburgh-bound.
Laurel-seeking he was, out of Orkney,
Long and salt his throat
Among the stanzas that starred the howffs of Rose Street.

Could he not bide forever in that beautiful city?
A sweet girl, one day,
Rose, a star, to greet him.
To him, she spoke sweeter than rain among roses in summer,
While poets like columns of salt stood
Round the oaken Abbotsford bar.
I, now
Going among the gray houses and piers of Stromness,
Hear that voice made of roses and rain still; and see
Through storm-clouds, the remembered star.

George Mackay Brown (1921–1996)

Some Things

D reaming
O f
O pen-plan
R ooms

H eaven
O rders
E arth

T hat
W hich
I s
N ext-to-nothing
E ndures

B estrides
A h!
L angorous
S ummer
A irs

Ian Hamilton Finlay

F   requent
L   ocal
O   ccasional
R   are
A   bundant

David Bellingham

Rehab No.6: (Shakespeare, Sonnet LV)

Piano tones . . . begin loud and bright
and then decay to silence in a complex way
that's characteristic of the instrument.
Robert Moog, Byte 6, 1986

Marrying clearest word to soundest verse
And five reiterations of the burden
Rowed in fire and stone (like a pharaoh's curse),
Intoned to last until the final Amen;
And we can't make head nor tail of who the song's
Regaling with its DECUS ET TUTAMEN.
Our end is nigh indeed if verse among
Stunned sinners is recalled when doom is clapping;
Absorb and sift, time, shift all that we've done,
Remit, maybe, a broken seal, Harappan
Inscription ◁ pan ⇧ -ar▤ ki(r), 'the singer's mark',
A thunderstone. Love doesn't fear the dark.

Peter McCarey

from Passacaglia on DSCH
for Dmitry Shostakovich

Ronald Stevenson
excerpt from Pars Tertia, Triple Fugue, Subj. II

51

A Poem Containing

Place Names
Catalogues
Found Poems
Variations

A Poem Containing

containing the word: launderette –
the words: finest equipment –
the words: oily overalls, horse tack and muddy
    sports gear you must not (repeat underlined
    must not) attempt to wash in these machines –
the words: load drum, amount detergent, add
    appropriate, desired wash, select cycle, coin
    in slot, proper amount, push slide, add before
    Rinse Light ON, again after Rinse Light OFF,
    not complete until Lid Light OUT (will not open
    until Lid Locked Light is also) –
then by pressing the words (it distinctly says
    pressing the words) High, Low, Permanent Press
    as required, ensure you follow in sequence the
    words to pre-set, then by pressing the word
    Start and re-pressing if need be –
each word as required, in sequence, expressing,
    resetting –
in words and with words: a launderette,
    containing a poem

Gael Turnbull

14:50 Rosekinghall
(Beeching Memorial Railway, Forfar Division)

The next train on Platform 6 will be the 14:50
Rosekinghall – Gallowshill and Blindwell, calling at:

Fairygreen – Templelands – Stars of Forthneth – Silverwells –
Honeyhole – Bee Cott – Pleasance – Sunnyblink –
Butterglen – Heatheryhaugh – St. Bride's Ring – Diltie Moss –
Silvie – Leyshade – Bourtreebush – Little Fithie –
Dusty Drum – Spiral Wood – Wandershiell – Windygates –
Red Roofs – Ark Hill – Egypt – Formal –
Letter – Laverockhall – Windyedge – Catchpenny –
Framedrum – Drumtick – Little Fardle – Packhorse –
Carrot – Clatteringbrigs – Smyrna – Bucklerheads –
Outfield – Jericho – Horn – Roughstones –
Loak – Skitchen – Sturt – Oathlaw –
Wolflaw – Farnought – Drunkendubs – Stronetic –
Ironharrow Well – Goats – Tarbrax – Dameye –
Dummiesholes – Caldhame – Hagmuir – Slug of Auchrannie –
Baldragon – Thorn – Wreaths – Spurn Hill –
Drowndubs – The Bloody Inches – Halfway – Groan,
where the train will divide

Don Paterson

Pool Poem

... The Bridge

The Cottage

Kay Braes

The Bend

Nicholson's Rock

The Castle

Garden wall

Slewans

Foghouse Nick

Chisholms

Segg Pool

Oak Strip

Maisondieu

Pothole

Annie End

Canty's cast

Try me Well

The Long Pool

The Wash Pool

Mill Pool

Gogaren

The Haughs

The Viaduct

Bloody Breeks

Quarry Pool

Sunlaws Mill

Turn Pool

Ninewells

Sandbed

Rock Cast ...

John Murray

Rose St	G3
Thistle St	G5
Lily St	G40
Myrtle Pl	G42
Daisy St	G42
Heather St	G41
Moss Rd	G51
Primrose St	G14
Yarrow Gdns	G20
Shamrock St	G4

Distance: approx. 12 miles

Chestnut St	G22
Acorn St	G40
Hazel Ave	G44
Mulberry Rd	G43
Walnut Cres	G22

Distance: approx. 10 miles

Souvenirs

A Selection of Street-Names
Adamsdown
Cardiff

Cone Incense
12 Kinds Assorted
Shoyeido & Co.
Kyoto

AGATE

CHERRY

COPPER

IRIS

DIAMOND

JASMINE

EMERALD

JONQUIL

GOLD

LILY

IRON

LOTUS

PEARL

PINE

PLATINUM

PLUM

RUBY

ROSE

SAPPHIRE

SANDALWOOD

SILVER

VIOLET

TOPAZ

WISTERIA

Ken Cockburn

Unsystematic Anatomy
After Rabelais

The vault of his cranium was an ordinary day shouting from the door
and his forehead was a drawer of objections
and his pineal was a big bellows
and his irises were Geminids on an bush evening
and his eardrums were tight skeins of geese
and the auricle of his ear a leaf stroked by Kafka in 1910
and his uvula was Benny Lynch's punchbag
and his saliva was a come-on
and his tongue was the negotiation of sweat-bath rituals.
His gullet was snake's knowledge
and his thyroid was the shield over Patroclus
and his recurrent laryngeal nerve was a prize-winning dissection
and his trachea was a ladder to the gods.
His spinal cord was all the news in sixty seconds.
His diaphragm was a bivouac on Cul Mor
and his lungs were the creature from the lagoon
and his liver was sitting all alone
and his gallbladder was the prodigal returning
and his mesentery was enough said about Boolahoola
and his spleen was the history of Belgium
and his stomach was pots and pans
and his small intestine the scarf that strangled Isadora Duncan.
His vena cava was the Third Man
and his mitral valve was a fond attachment
and his aorta was the Twenty-Third Psalm sung in the Hebrides
and his heart was an artichoke.
His kidneys were Pliny on recycling
and his ureters were double bungee jumpers reclining
and his bladder was a seat at the Citz watching the Chalk Circle

and his spermatic cords were a strung violin
and his penis was done on a dare.
His hips were titanium-vanadium, where the angel touched,
and his perineum was a canvas big top
and his pelvis was Lear's fool
and his femurs were a dream of being next in command
and his calves were pay first, touch later
and one foot was a Lisbon lion
and the other took a while.

His memory was laminar germ theory
and his commonsense was seasick in the heart of Europe
and his imagination was an open cast
and his thoughts were English composition and rhetoric
and his conscience was a lease on a bird cage in the Walled City
and his appetite was Boswell's inkhorn
and his hope was one for the road
and his undertakings were Daedalus and Icarus in the maze
and his will was the Cape of Good Hope
and his desire was the wounds of possibility
and his judgement was Solomon's treatises on deep tongues
and his compassion was undergrowth
and his discretion was beached, between herring and seaweed
and his reason sat down to turn itself in

in the gap between the boyhood burning of his ears
and finally arriving as himself.

Iain Bamforth

from Pantagruel

How Epistemon, who had his head cut off, was finely healed by Panurge, and of the news which he brought from the Devils, and of the damned People in Hell.

... in respect of the damned, [Epistemon] said he was very sorry, that Panurge had so soon called him back into this world again; for, said he, I took wonderful delight to see them. How so? said Pantagruel. Because they do not use them there, said Epistemon, so badly as you think they do. Their estate and condition of living is but only changed after a very strange manner; for I saw Alexander the Great there, mending and patching on clouts upon old breeches and stockings, and thus got a very poor living.

Xerxes was a crier of mustard.
Romulus, a salter and patcher of pattens.
Numa, a nailsmith.
Tarquin, a porter.
Piso, a clownish swain.
Sylla, a ferryman.
Cyrus, a cowherd.
Themistocles, a glass-maker.
Epaminondas, a maker of mirrors or looking-glasses.
Brutus and Cassius, surveyors or measurers of land.
Demosthenes, a vine-dresser.
Cicero, a fire-kindler.
Fabius, a threader of beads.
Artaxerxes, a rope-maker.
Aeneas, a miller.
Achilles was a scald-pated maker of hay-bundles.
Agamemnon, a lick-box.

Ulysses, a hay-mower.

Nestor, a deer-keeper or forester.

Darius, a gold-finder, or jakes-farmer.

Ancus Martius, a ship-trimmer.

Camillus, a foot-post.

Marcellus, a sheller of beans.

Drusus, a taker of money at the doors of play-houses.

Scipio Africanus, a crier of lee in a wooden-slipper.

Asdrubal, a lantern-maker.

Hannibal, a kettle-maker and seller of egg shells.

Priamus, a seller of old clouts.

Lancelot of the Lake was a flayer of dead horses.

All the knights of the Round Table, were poor day-labourers, employed
to row over the rivers of Cocytus, Phlegeton, Styx, Acheron, and
Lethe, when my lords the devils had a mind to recreate themselves
upon the water, as in the like occasion are hired the boatmen at
Lyons, the gondoliers of Venice, and oars of London. But with this
difference, that these poor knights have only for their fare a bob or
flirt on the nose, and, in the evening, a morsel of coarse mouldy
bread.

Trajan was a fisher of frogs.

Antoninus, a lackey.

Commodus, a bagpiper.

Pertinax, a peeler of walnuts.

Lucullus, a maker of rattles and hawks' bells.

Justinian, a pedlar.

Hector, a snap-sauce scullion.

Paris was a poor beggar.

Cambyses, a mule driver.

Nero, a base blind fiddler, or player on that instrument which is called a wind-broach. Fierabras was his serving-man, who did him a thousand mischievous tricks, and would make him eat of the brown bread, and drink of the turned wine, when himself did both eat and drink of the best.

Julius Caesar and Pompey were boat-wrights and tighters of ships.

Valentine and Orson did serve in the stoves of hell, and were sweat-rubbers in hot houses.

Giglan and Gawain were poor swine-herds.

Geoffrey with the great tooth, was a tinder-maker and seller of matches.

Godfrey de Bullion, a hood-maker.

Jason was a bracelet-maker.

Don Pietro de Castille, a carrier of indulgences.

Morgante, a beer-brewer.

Huon of Bordeaux, a hooper of barrels.

Pyrrhus, a kitchen-scullion.

Antiochus, a chimney-sweeper.

Octavian, a scraper of parchment.

Nerva, a mariner.

Pope Julius was a crier of pudding-pies, but he left off wearing there his great buggerly beard.

John of Paris was a greaser of boots.

Arthur of Britain, an ungreaser of caps.

Perce-Forest, a carrier of fagots.

Pope Boniface the Eighth, a scummer of pots.

Pope Nicholas the Third, a maker of paper.

Pope Alexander, a rat-catcher.

Pope Sixtus, an anointer of those that have the pox . . .

Pope Calixtus was a barber of a woman's *sine quo non*.

Pope Urban, a bacon-picker.

Melusina was a kitchen drudge-wench.

Matabrune, a laundress.

Cleopatra, a crier of onions.

Helen, a broker for chamber-maids.

Semiramis, the beggars' lice-killer.

Dido did sell mushrooms.

Penthesilea sold cresses.

Lucretia was an ale-house keeper.

Hortensia, a spinstress.

Livia, a grater of verdgrease.

François Rabelais (1494–1553)
translated by Sir Thomas Urquhart (1612–1660).

Apple Blossoms, Eastwards of Motherwell, 1806

Nothing asked, and nobody, nobody to cast clouds.
Day trippers come eastwards, by rail and coach, an annual outing
to Eden. Nothing but apple blossom, rippling Clyde, clear blue sky
and defining swifts. Nothing of the flaming sword
turning every way to guard the path to the Tree of Life. Nothing of
low flying planes casting chemicals. Nobody there to question that
Tree of Knowledge, of Good and Evil. The nameable varieties
are defining that 1806 world, eastwards of Motherwell,

Early and Summer: Junetine, amber,
chucket-egg,
lady apple, lady's lemon, summer strawberry,
Milford, American pippin,
kailbed,
Dryly pippin, gairien, &c.

Middle or harvest: white cluster, queen of England,
white Ledington, bloodheart, Dumbarton pippin,
whistleberry,
salmon, common codling, lemon pippin, Hamilton pippin,
Moncrieff, marrow,
lady's finger, &c.

Late or Winter: Yorkshire greening, nonpareil,
green Ledington, gray Ledington, winter strawberry,
golden pippin, pearmain apple, Hawthornden,
naked apple,
nonesuch, green cluster, green calender, Ely, Falwood,
golden Monday, grass-apple, redstreak, coalhouse,

and
Corstorphine, sheephead,
Carse of Gowrie,
pursemouth, royal codlin, and several
sorts
of russets.

Now we come, and how,
nothing but guide-book tourists grasping at memories,
trailing particles of oil. Modified answers are given
before we ask the subtle serpent why, and again why,
why the orchards are cleared. And glimpse

two dead trees in that garden westward of genetic thickets.

Duncan Glen

the fool's   the one-rowed   watercress

the brackish   the chalk-stream   the common   the fan-leaved   the pond
the river   the thread-leaved   water crowfoot

the corky-fruited   the fine-leaved   the hemlock   the narrow-leaved
the parsley   the river   the tubular   water dropwort

the fringed   the least   the white   the yellow   water lily

the alternate   the spiked   the whorled   water milfoil

the greater   the lesser   water parsnip

the small   the tasteless   water pepper

the common   the floating   the lesser   the narrow-leaved
the Parnassus-leaved   the ribbon-leaved   water plantain

the curly   the greater   the large-flowered   water thyme

water wort

Gerry Loose

Carefree

Belinda
Kathleen
Frau Dagmar Hastrup

D. Stemler, *The Book of Old Roses*, 1966

Pavel Büchler

mileanach
fearsaideach
eireleag
saimbhir
liath-lus na tràghad

meilbheag

an raineach mhòr

droigheann
cuileann
caorann

roid
beithe
lus nam braoileag
bunglas
fraoch

giuthas

zostera maritima
cakile maritima
atriplex littoralis
crithmum maritima
plantago mariima

papaver rhoeas

pteridium aquilinum

crataegus
ilex aquifolium
sorbus aucuparia

myrica gale
betula
vaccinium vitis-idaea
molinia caerulea
calluna vulgaris

pinus sylvestris

herman de vries

Eleven Sea Anemones and One Coral

Snakelocks   Beadlet   Dahlia

Burrowing   Strawberry   Cloak

Plumose   Gem   Daisy

Parasitic   Jewel   Cup

Eleven Crabs and One Goby

Hairy	Edible	Hermit
Spider	Porcelain	Masked
Swimming	Spiny	Thornback
Velvet	Shore	Black

World Cup Teams
Scotland

FR 214
ANCHOR OF HOPE

KY 136   BK 20   AH 98   FH 16
HOPE   BRAW LADS   GUIDING STAR   TRY AGAIN

FR 47   LT 277   BA 158   LK 192
GOOD INTENT   VALIANT STAR   SILVER LINING   SWIFTWING II

FY 128   LH 116
BAND OF HOPE   GOOD HOPE

SUBSTITUTES:
PD 70 STAR OF PROMISE,
KY 327 BRIGHTER HOPE III,
KY 357 CONTENDER,
PD 217 RIVAL,
AH 120 NEW ERA

MANAGER: PD 477 OUR GUIDE
COACH: ME 89 WHISPERING HOPE

Alec Finlay

74

From the Rete of a Gothic Astrolabe

COR LEONIS
(KEEPER)

HUMERUS EQUE   ALA EQUI   CAPUT ALGOL   ALDEBORA

RYGYL   ALBABOR   ALRAMECH   VULTER CADENS

ARIOS   CORONA ELFECA

ELEVEN STAR NAMES FROM THE RETE OF A GOTHIC ASTROLABE:
MUSEUM BOERHAAVE, LEIDEN: INV. NR. 3102
BRASS. UNSIGNED AND UNDATED
MAKER UNKNOWN (POSSIBLY FRENCH); CIRCA1450

Kevin Henderson

from Empty Quarter

             this night when we reached camp.
So we passed on

                                    in various parts of the desert.
We marched on

             with larger fragments of rock.
From this basin-tract

almost starless sky.
I awoke before dawn

to break the silence of the desert.

Despite the long and strenuous journey

                              upon the site.
The valley now ran

  hither we had come.
A hare –

the bed of an ancient lake or lagoon.

Beyond it west

white in the hazy sunshine.
Here lay Turaiwa

of call for casual travellers.

We had now

sands – white or blue-grey in colouring.

About 10 miles west

Jim Harold

The Grey Line

Blue in the face, grey haired

grey goose mother, lend me thy wings

grey and lifeless-looking

grown grey

the iron-grey gravel flats, the sombre mountain

the grey darkness outside

in the grey light of dawn

clear eyes, hard and cold grey

grey as yet

thin wisps of grey

grey of broken iron

grey and flaccid

grey streaked

grey with hay mould

a dapple grey head

glides the grey gull crying above

soft blue-grey

lonely and grey, with fewer and fewer birds

the grey-spotted calf

tufted on one, grey-spotted on another

whose grey-blue eyes were complacent

in the grey light of the morning

grey-striped and suspicious

they understood the grey in each other

he had grey

early in March a grey light beginning to show
a grey indeterminate dawn
still so grey on the window
grey and sick
in the dim, grey-blue light
on the river's grey, unruffled pools
pretty grey
silver grey
grey
grey
grey summer
grey
grey
grey
the moss was grey and the withered grass white
grey
grey
the grey on the skyline

Donald Urquhart
from *Independent People* by Halldór Laxness

Perfect

On the Western Seaboard of South Uist
(Los muertos abren los ojos a los que viven)

I found a pigeon's skull on the machair,
All the bones pure white and dry, and chalky,
But perfect,
Without a crack or a flaw anywhere.

At the back, rising out of the beak,
Were twin domes like bubbles of thin bone,
Almost transparent, where the brain had been
That fixed the tilt of the wings.

Hugh MacDiarmid (1892–1978)
after Glyn Jones

Kennst Du

Do you know the sea where the lemon-shaped fishing boats rock? Softly, in the shadowy stern, the orange net-floats shine. A salt wind stirs the sail, a silver fountain springs from the vessel's side. Beloved, did you know this sea? Did you know it well?

Kennst du das Land, wo die Zitronen blühn, / Im dunkeln Laub die Gold-Orangen glühn, / Ein sanfter Wind vom blauen Himmel weht, / Die Myrte still und hoch der Lorbeer steht, / Kennst du es wohl? Dahin! Dahin / Möcht ich mit dir, o mein Geleibter, ziehn.

Ian Hamilton Finlay
Johann Wolfgang von Goethe (1749–1832)

A Good Warfare

Thank you for your excellent letter,
very like yourself, most letters
are not like men at all but like other letters,
though my time occupied with various forms of
nothing, a poor wanderer on this earth,
the faculty of blundering growing upon me,
having a constant succession of visitors
of all varieties, with much wear to mind
and body, yet many whom I love
for that activity in their friendship
of heart and intellect, contending for reality
against shadows which is always a good warfare,

for many speculate on religion,
not with the desire of arriving at truth
but of finding arguments for opinion,
inflicting desolation and paralysis, though He is
indeed far above all doctrines, Whose thoughts
are not as ours, and the cry of a child
will produce a greater movement in almost any mind
than twenty pages of unanswerable logic

but that God should be omnipotent love
and yet the world be a vast cauldron
of violence, pollution, misery, is a riddle,
and the seeming triumph of darkness over light,
a riddle. We have our being in the midst
of what encloses us as a net
on every hand, and among the many marvels

in man's character and condition,
few greater than this, that he should be able
to contemplate his situation without astonishment,
which is indeed, a mighty riddle, God's riddle,
and none can solve it but God

whom I desire to know as really –
and far more – as I know any man, for
it is not by thoughts that I am to be comforted.
I desire and expect an actual putting forth
of His hand, a direct breathing of His love.
I should like to be able to receive
all the sorrows and pains of life, as it were,
by the kiss of God. Dear friend, I find
that I had entirely forgotten
who it was that I was writing to . . .

Gael Turnbull
from various letters and writings by Thomas Erskine of Linlathen (1788–1870)

Secrets Seen

Pattern Poems
Shape Poems

OF JET,
Or PORPHYRIE,
Or that white Stone,
Paros affoordes alone,
Or these in AZURE dye,
Which seem to scorne the SKYE;
Here Memphis Wonders doe not set,
Nor ARTEMESIA'S huge Frame,
That keepes so long her Lovers Name:
Make no great marble Atlas tremble with Gold
To please a Vulgar EYE that doth beholde.
The Muses, Phoebus, Love, have raised of their teares
A Crystal Tomb to Him wherethrough his worth appears.

William Drummond (1585–1649)

Nelson's Column

I
the
rim
y cl
ouds
ascen
d , —
R e n d
ye po
rtals o
f the s
k y , —
Flee to
every d
istant la
nd,— T
o celebr
ate his *m*
emory!—
Trump -
ets blow
from pol
e to pole!
—R o c k s
& w o o d s
your ech
o e s   j o i n ;
— T h r o'
the vallies
m a k e   t h e -
m   r o l l , —
A n d   w r e a
ths of mus
ic for him
t w i n e . —
See! the HE
RO mounts aloft,
Palms and gar
lands Angel's
bring;—Tune your tim
brels sweet and soft,
Of the seas pro
claim him KING:
—Tho' no mort
al crown he wo
re,—*Nelson* no
w immortal rei
g n s , — T r a v e r s
ings winds the deeps expl
ore,—And strew his GLO
RIES o'er the plains,—And when Hi
storians' pages cease—To tell of mighty
deeds in war,—My never-ending them is this,—
THE GLORIOUS VICTORY OF TRAFALGAR!

George MacIndoe (1771–1848)

Islam

min
a
ret
place
of
fire
pharos
beacon
light
beckoning
the faithful
five times
a day
on and off
flashing
and
filtered
through carved
mashrabeya
of the night

purifies
mind's light
of reason

lifts
pointed
slender
stem
of feeling

cleaves
the sky
spiralling
like smoke

above the domed
house of gathered
living

above the court
yard
of cleansed hearts

above pillared
terraces of prayer

where forehead
stoops to dent
hallowed dust
and palms open
holding nothing back

through minaret
like lightning
conducted

FLAMES
ONE
TRUE THOUGHT

ALLAH!

Tessa Ransford

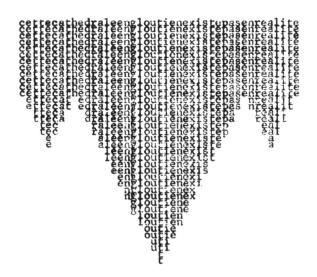

```
maisilya                        s
maisilya                        o
maisilya                       esq
maisilya                       lesqu
maisilya                      lesqui
maisilya                     alesqui
maisilya                     alesqui
maisilyadautrescathedralesquirefletentleurs
maisilyadautrescathedralesquirefletentleursim
maisilyadautrescathedralesquirefletentleursima
maisilyadautrescathedralesquirefletentleursimag
maisilyadautrescathedralesquirefletentleursimages
maisilyadautrescathedralesquirefletentleursimages
maisilyadautrescathedralesquirefletentleursimages
maisilyadautrescathedralesquirefletentleursimages
maisilyadautrescathedralesquirefletentleursimages
maisilyadautrescathedralesquirefletentleursimages
maisilyadautrescathedralesquirefletentleursimages
maisilyadautrescathedralesquirefletentleursimages
maisilyadautrescathedralesquirefletentleursimages
maisilyadautrescathedralesquirefletentleursimages
maisilyadautrescathedralesquirefletentleursimages
maisilyadautrescathedralesquirefletentleursimages
maisilyadautrescathedralesquirefletentleursimages
maisilyadautrescathedralesquirefletentleursimages
maisilyadautrescathedralesquirefletentleursimages
maisilyadautrescathedralesquirefletentleursimages
maisilyadautrescathedralesquirefletentleursimages
maisilyadautrescathedralesquirefletentleursimages
maisilyadautrescathedralesquirefletentleursimages
maisilyadautrescathedralesquirefletentleursi
maisilya                     alesqui
maisilya                     alesqui
maisilya                      lesqu
maisilya                       esq
maisilya                        o
maisilya                        s
maisilya
```

Alan Riddell (1927–1977)

Pomander

pomander
open pomander
open poem and her
open poem and him
open poem and hymn
hymn and hymen leander
high man pen meander
o pen poem me and her
pen me poem me and him
om mane padme hum
pad me home panda hand
open up o holy pandhandler
ample panda pen or bamboo pond
ponder a bonny poem pomander opener
open banned peon penman hum and banter
open hymn and pompom band and panda hamper
o i am a pen open man or happener
i am open manner happener
happy are we open
poem and a pom
poem and a pand a
poem and aplomb

Edwin Morgan

LILIES

Ivory white on
Bronze and green
Float on the amber
Waters of lochans
Lone.
Are they gleaming nipples of nymphs unseen,
Lost Ophelias man shall never own?

Evening
Seals with silver
Their beauty rare,
Rooted deep in the silt
Of a thousand
Years.
Only the bending reeds in the moonlight fair
Whisper of secrets seen; but no one hears.

Helen B. Cruickshank (1886–1975)

RUDDER

p
i
t
c
h

on

pine

this rudder has cheeks from pitch-pine, salvaged from a skip outside a church
and fastened to white-painted spruce

Ian Stephen

Do Gheas
Spell

Cha dèan do gheas mo leas. Ach tha mi coma 's mi an comas Air sìneadh sìos air leabaidh-fhlocais, 'S mo chneas a' sineadh ri do chneas.

Your spell won't do me any good
but I don't care so long as I'm able
to snuggle with you under the downie,
my skin stretched out over yours.

Rody Gorman

98

from Heraclitean Variations

its work is death

Ian Hamilton Finlay

nora's place nora's

place nora's place

nora's place nora's

place nora's place

nora's place nora's

place nora's place

nora's place nora's

place nora's place

nora's place nora's

place nora's place

nora's place nora's

place nora's place

nora's place
nora's place
nora's place
nora's place
nora's place
nora's place
nora's place
nora's place
nora's place
nora's place   nora's place   nora's place nora's place
nora's place   nora's place   nora's place nora's place
nora's place   nora's place   nora's place nora's place

nora's place nora's place
nora's place nora's place
nora's place nora's place

Tom Leonard

Black Block

Futurism
Fauvism
Suprematism

Alerting

'. . . that this book, too, has made some difference, by alerting western students of literature to . . .' Victor Erlich (*Russian Formalism*)

RING TALE

Ting Lear –
Ireglant
Gaeltrin
Eringalt
Relating
trigenal,
algetrin,
geanitrl:
regal nit.

Tal Niger
alerting
Ting Lear –
Tengrila
ten grail
glint. Are
near gilt,
argentli
gliteran.

Tal Niger
gent – liar:
intreagl.
Tengrila –
Tigerlan,
Grinleat.
Itler? Gna!
Atilr? Neg! –

GIANTLER,
angritel.

l . . . granite
graintle.

Grait nel:
Ting Lear,
nil targe,
eg train
Tengrila,
neg trail
(Irtlegan,
Geantirl,
Liartgen).

GIANTLER
Lint rage.
Ear tingl,
a-trengil,
Ting Lear –
gnat. Rile
GIANTLER.
"Ent…grail."
"Gralient!"
"Large tin"
"Argle nit!"
"Large tin?"

"Lager tin.
Rentagil."

Ting Lear
alert. Gin.
Gin. Alter.
Eartl gin
gin. Tra-le!
Regal Nit
leg tiran.
Lartigen!
Gin. Arlet. . .
Ting Lear
a-trengil.
"R, eligant".
Rae glint;
Entragil?
Neat girl,
girt, neal.
Genitral.
Genitalr.
Galentri.
Inert gal.

entir-Alg!
GIANTLER!

Ting Lear,
great nil:
nil targe,
lager tin.
Ran gilte.

Neg trail,
Lrit Naeg,
Nag eltri,
Liart Gen,
Alirgnet,
Eringalt,
Gaeltrin.

Altering
Tengrila
(Giantler –
liar. Gent –
ril agent),
Ting Lear
alerting
Ireglant
girn late,
relating
integral
ringtale

Peter McCarey

Ha-oo! ha-oo! ha-oo!
Many of the black ones
Ha-oo! ha-oo! ha-oo!
Dogs of the rebellion
Ha-oo! ha-oo! ha-oo!
Scampered through the snow
Ha-oo! ha-oo! ha-oo!
To the nearby villages
Ha-oo! ha-oo! ha-oo!
To root up all the corpses
Ha-oo! ha-oo! ha-oo!
To drag off someone's leg
Ha-oo! ha-oo! ha-oo!
To drag off someone's arm
Ha-oo! ha-oo! ha-oo!
To bloody up their muzzles
In belly and in snow.

Song of the lips – bobeóbi,
Song of the eyes – veeómi,
Song of the eyebrows – pieéo,
Song of the look – lieeéi,
Song of the chain – gzi-gzi-gzéo.
So, on the canvas of such correspondences
A Portrait, living in no dimension.

Velimir Khlebnikov (1885–1922)
translated by Edwin Morgan

you were a good girl to me
    worr o guid gurl ti ma
you were a good   to me
        o guid gurl   ma
you were   to me
        o guid gurl
you were   to
       gui gurl
you were

                ti ma
      good   to
        gurl
   worr   gui   ti
         to
            ma

Ernst Jandl (1925–2000)
translated by Edwin Morgan

First Suprematist Standing Poem

how blue!
how far!
how sad!
how small!
how white!

how blue?
how sad?
how small?
how white?
how far?

Homage to Malevich

```
l  a  c  k  b  l  o  c  k  b  l  a  c  k  b
l  o  c  k  b  l  a  c  k  b  l  o  c  k  b
l  a  c  k  b  l  o  c  k  b  l  a  c  k  b
l  o  c  k  b  l  a  c  k  b  l  o  c  k  b
l  a  c  k  b  l  o  c  k  b  l  a  c  k  b
l  o  c  k  b  l  a  c  k  b  l  o  c  k  b
l  a  c  k  b  l  o  c  k  b  l  a  c  k  b
l  o  c  k  b  l  a  c  k  b  l  o  c  k  b
l  a  c  k  b  l  o  c  k  b  l  a  c  k  b
l  o  c  k  b  l  a  c  k  b  l  o  c  k  b
l  a  c  k  b  l  o  c  k  b  l  a  c  k  b
l  o  c  k  b  l  a  c  k  b  l  o  c  k  b
l  a  c  k  b  l  o  c  k  b  l  a  c  k  b
```

Ian Hamilton Finlay

Cluster
for Eugen Gomringer

CON^STELLA^TION
^CENTRA

Icon
for Kasimir Malevich

BL^A^CK
^O

from Palabrar*mas*

*Wurdwappin*schaw

per_{mite}
el dón

gie
for
gie

ver_{dad}
dad_{ver}

oan_{esty}
stey_{oan}

Cecilia Vicuña
translated by Edwin Morgan

From Deep to Deep

from deep
to deep
from near
to near
from grey
to grey
from deep
to near
from near
to grey
from grey
to deep

from two
to four
from three
to one
from one
to four

from deep
to two
from four
to near
from grey
to one

Eugen Gomringer
translated by Edwin Morgan

Ballad

ballad
ballad

    brooded
    brooded
    brooded
        beloved
        beloved
            bird
            bird
            bird
                ballad
                brooded
                beloved
                    bird

Edgard Braga (1897–1985)
translated by Edwin Morgan

isle
smile

tranquil

Edgard Braga (1897–1985)
translated by Edwin Morgan

The Order of Things

Concrete Poems
Constellations

Ian Hamilton Finlay

star
star
star
star
star
star
star
star
star
star
star
steer

Sea Poppy 2

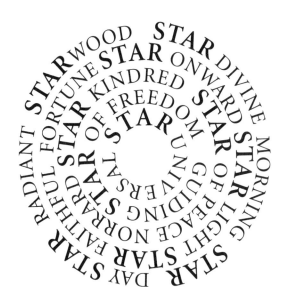

Ian Hamilton Finlay

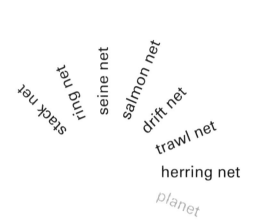

stack net
ring net
seine net
salmon net
drift net
trawl net
herring net
planet

ring of waves

row of nets

string of lights

row of fish

ring of nets

row of roofs

string of fish

ring of light

Ian Hamilton Finlay

Gorse
goRse
gOrse
roUse
gorSe
gorsE

d
n d r
i n d r o
a i n d r o p
r a i n d r o p s

```
this
  little      i
thistle   h    s
        t    i    t    e
          l    t    l              i
        t    i    t    e    h    s
           h    s    l    t    i    t    e
                               l    t    l
                          t    i    t    e
                          h    s    l
```



```
        rookSHEEP
        MOONstack
        rockSHEEP
        NOONstack
        rookSHAPE
        MOONstook
        rockSHAPE
        NOONstook
```

Ronald Johnson (1935–1998)

The Honey Pot

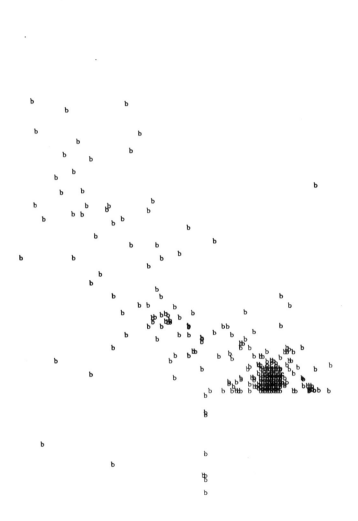

Alan Riddell (1927–1977)

The Chaffinch Map of Scotland

                    chaffinch
                 chaffinchaffinch
            chaffinchaffinchaffinch
            chaffinchaffinchaffinch
               chaffinchaffinch
                    chaffinch
              chaffie   chye   chaffiechaffie
              chaffie   chye   chaffiechaffie
                         chye chaffie
                 chaffiechaffiechaffie
                 chaffiechaffiechaffie
                     chaffiechaffie
                     chaffiechaffie
                     chaffiechaffie
                     chaffiechaffie

                   shilly shelly
              shelfyshilfyshellyshilly
                 shelfyshillyshilly
                 shilfyshellyshelly
               shilfyshelfyshelly
                      shellyfaw
                  shielyshellyfaw
           shilfy
           shilfyshelfy shielyshiely
      shilfyshelfyshelfy   shielychaffie
           chaffiechaffie   chaffiechaffie
           chaffiechaffie
        shilfyshilfyshilfyshelfyshelfy
     chaffieshilfyshilfyshelfyshelfyshelfyshelfy
     chaffieshilfyshilfyshelfyshelfyshelfyshelfyshelfy
        shilfyshilfyshilfyshelfy   shelfyshelfy
        shilfy   shilfy
                shilfy
                shilfyshelfy

brichtie

Siesta of a Hungarian Snake

s   sz   sz   SZ   sz   SZ   sz   ZS   zs   ZS   zs   zs   z

Edwin Morgan

Two Gardens

Max Planck Institute, Stuttgart
Little Sparta, Lanarkshire

Ian Hamilton Finlay

Max Planck Institute
Photographs by Werner J. Hannappel

Little Sparta
Photographs by Robin Gillanders

Acrobats

Grids
Nets
Matrices

The Honest Farmer's Declaration

Printed verbatim from his own mouth.

```
t o R e h T t n a n t T h e R o t
o R e h T t n a W a n t T h e R o
R e h T t n a W a W a n t T h e R
e h T t n a W a n a W a n t T h e
h T t n a W a n n n a W a n t T h
T t n a W a n n a n n a W a n t T
t n a W a n n a C a n n a W a n t
n a W a n n a C e C a n n a W a n
a W a n n a C e W e C a n n a W a
n a W a n n a C e C a n n a W a n
t n a W a n n a C a n n a W a n t
T t n a W a n·n a n n a W a n t T
h T t n a W a n n n a W a n t T h
e h T t n a W a n a W a n t T h e
R e h T t n a W a W a n t T h e R
o R e h T t n a W a n t T h e R o
t o R e h T t n a n t T h e R o t


t n e R e h T h e R e n t
n e R e h T s T h e R e n
e R e h T s y s T h e R e
R e h T s y a y s T h e R
e h T s y a P a y s T h e
h T s y a P t P a y s T h
T s y a P t I t P a y s T
h T s y a P t P a y s T h
e h T s y a P a y s T h e
R e h T s y a y s T h e R
e R e h T s y s T h e R e
n e R e h T s T h e R e n
t n e R e h T h e R e n t
```

Anon (1853)

Homage to Dom Silvester Houédard

typewriter scaffolding typewriter scaffolding typewriter scaffolding typewriter scaffolding typewriter scaffolding typewriter scaffolding typewriter scaffolding typewriter

David Bellingham

a   a   a   a   a
 c   c   c   c
r   r   r   r   r
 o   o   o   o
b   b   b   b   b
 a   a   a   a
t   t   t   t   t
 s   s   s   s
t   t   t   t   t
 a   a   a   a
b   b   b   b   b
 o   o   o   o
r   r   r   r   r
 c   c   c   c
a   a   a   a   a

Ian Hamilton Finlay

Safety Net for Practice Tower

dare   devil   trap-

air   grace   ease

faultless   falter   fall

Alastair Fowler

loved	by	her	eyes
by	**face**	**into**	loved
her	**a**	**wall**	by
eyes	loved	by	her

loved	by	her	eyes
by	**not**	**here**	loved
her	**not**	**there**	by
eyes	loved	by	her

loved	by	her	eyes
by	**some**	**visible**	loved
her	**at**	**night**	by
eyes	loved	by	her

Kevin Henderson

tendressetendressetendressetendressetend
erdresstenderdresstenderdresstenderdress
tenderdresstenderdresstenderdresstenderd
ressetendressetendressetendressetendress
etenderderesstenderdresstenderdresstender
dressetendressetendressetendressetendres
setendressetendressetendressetendressete
nderdresstenderdresstenderdresstenderdre
ssetendressetendressetendressetendresset
enderdresstenderdresstenderdresstenderdr
essetendressetendressetendressetendresse

Mandala: Dilemma

Alastair Reid

Dehiscence

jibe

pea

forge

an

to

is

sees

whom

two

a

apt

via

won

chore

nub

prig

ray

oat

to

amp

net

out

on

on

Thomas Evans

Blue Happening Theatre

Permutations
Emergent Poems

UNITED
UNLIED

LUCID
LUCID

Alan Woods (1956–2000)

A Flower for Andreas Gryphius (1616–1664)
Ornithogalum umbellatum

```
s
st
 sta
star
  star-
  star-o
    star-of
    star-of-
       star-of-b
       star-of-be
           star-of-bet
           star-of-beth
               star-of-bethl
               star-of-bethle
                   star-of-bethleh
                   star-of-bethlehe
                       star-of-bethlehem
                             tar-of Bethlehem
                             ar-of-bethlehem
                                   r-of-bethlehem
                                    -of bethlehem
                                        of-bethlehem
                                        f-bethlehem
                                            -bethlehem
                                            bethlehem
                                               ethlehem
                                               thlehem
                                                   hlehem
                                                   lehem
                                                      ehem
                                                      hem
                                                         em
                                                         m
```

Ken Cockburn

```
F U R R O W
U R R O W S
R R O W S O
R O W S O R
O W S O R R
W S O R R O
S O R R O W
O R R O W F
R R O W F U
R O W F U R
O W F U R R
W F U R R O
F U R R O W
```

```
F A L L O W
A L L O W H
L L O W H A
L O W H A L
O W H A L L
W H A L L O
H A L L O W
A L L O W F
L L O W F A
L O W F A L
O W F A L L
W F A L L O
F A L L O W
```

Thomas A. Clark

Outward Bound
(emergent poem for Edwin Morgan)

```
                      l        ook
         is     f    ate like
th    is
             o  r
th               at
                         a
t    re                  e
         is
                 a          book
         is                 a
               gate
 here is  o     a     k
 there is        t     e a     k
                g                o
t         o
      s           e      a
t              a    ke
ther  is                         k
          o f  ga    l   e
          o fr   at
  e               at
              f  ig
 he               at
      s          a     ke
 h        o                    ok
   e                 e l
     re  s          t
t               a    ke
t  e                      a
          o  r
                          a book
the     s   o f    t  li  e
there            at  l
          no f   a    ke
          no fr    e      a      k
          s            e    e
there is no frigate like a book
```

Hamish Whyte
derived from a line by Emily Dickinson

Seven Headlines

```
                ol                 d
                sol      e    m        n
                  o                de
                sol                d
      f               o                    r
      f    e              n    der
  i      r    o                    n
              b  ol              d
          tre            n    d
  i                      n
      l     et                t    er
                             t   o
                sol              o
          re a                   der
      a     r    so    n
  i                                n
              b  ol     t
      f     r    o   m
              b   lu   e
      a         bs    ent
      f               o        od
              b    u        d
      f           o  u    n    d
       ut  t e                         r
      f    e r        ment
  i                      n
          re a  so                     n
          t e a    m
      f    e  e                      d
      a    t                 modern
                    l            ode
                    n    o
      f    et            t    er
      f            o                   r
          absolu    t      e
                    m    odern
                    men
il faut être absolument moderne
```

Edwin Morgan
derived from a line by Arthur Rimbaud

Variations from Sappho

1.

mingled with all manner of colours
mingled withall manner of colours
minglad with allmanner of colours
mengladwith all mingled of colours
man glad withall mangled of colours
manglad with all mingle of call ours

2.

        heart   altogether
I can   shine back
              shall be to me
              shall be to me
        heart   altogether
I can   shine back

3.

It is not you who are to me
it is   who are to me
   is not
        you who are
              to me
it is not   me
        who?

4.

You burn me
Yu   born my
  o   u   y
You bore me
   w   h   y

5.

a(ll) mi(xed)
te(ll) tongue (me)
tell to(ngue) ( )
t(all)
les(s)

Veronica Forrest-Thomson (1947–1975)

from In the Slums of Glasgow

I am filled forever with a glorious awareness
Of the inner radiance, the mystery of the hidden light in these dens,
I see it glimmering like a great white-sailed ship
Bearing into Scotland from Eternity's immense,
Or like a wild swan resting a moment in mid-flood.
It has the air of a winged victory, in suspense
By its own volition in its imperious way.
As if the heavens opened I gather its stupendous sense.

For here too, Philosophy has a royal and ancient seat,
And, holding an eternal citadel of light and immortality,
With Study her only comrade, sets her victorious foot
On the withering flower of the fast-ageing world. – Let all men see.

Now the babel of Glasgow dies away in our ears,
The great heart of Glasgow is sinking to rest,
Na nonanunno nunnono nana nananana nanu
Nunno nunnonanunneno nanena nunnanunnanut.
We lie cheek to cheek in a quiet trance, the moon itself no more still.
There is no movement but your eyelashes fluttering against me,
And the fading sound of the work-a-day world,
Dadadoduddadaddadi dadadodudadidadoh,
Duddadam dadade dudde dadadadadadodadah.

Hugh MacDiarmid (1892–1978)

From the Sanskrit

'We give an example of an ekaksara stanza,
employing only one consonant throughout:

Dadado dudda-dud-dadi
dadado duda-di-da-doh
dud-dadam dadade dudde
dad'-adada-dado 'da-dah'

Did I do Dido? Wd I dodo
DD? Do IOU a dead id?
D-day, de-wedded, I did dhow.
'Aid Dido, dude', ode daddy added,
Aideed'd aid Aida'. Da?
You'd owe a dewy-eyed ode, ide oid.
Adieu. A dowdy odd doe O-D'd.

Peter McCarey

Festive Permutation Poem-Happening for Brighton

green symphony terrace
tasty sea kite
gay pavilion cats
gold sport orchestra
lazy cloud theatre
loud boat bucket
blowy spring roundabout
new crash guitar
tingling sand diva
blue pier eels
happy cake poetry
cool bunting happening
huge candyfloss birds
mellow steak music
hopping art dogs
red sun scene
jellied transistor show
high fish dance

huge poetry boat
gay pier steak
cool kite theatre
green sea cats
blowy transistor birds
new eels orchestra
mellow cloud show
hopping dance candyfloss
high dogs happening
tingling bucket terrace
tasty bunting symphony
jellied diva scene
gold roundabout art
loud sand cake
happy spring fish
red crash music
lazy sport sun
blue guitar pavilion

gold sea diva

tasty bunting sport

green kite symphony

lazy crash bucket

blue boat birds

gay candyfloss music

huge spring steak

tingling sun cake

jellied guitar happening

high eels show

happy cats pier

hopping fish scene

mellow sand dance

cool art orchestra

new transistor pavilion

loud cloud roundabout

red theatre dogs

blowy poetry terrace

happy cloud theatre

cool eels scene

mellow dogs orchestra

red art roundabout

blue spring happening

hopping pier sport

huge diva dance

green fish poetry

lazy birds pavilion

gay candyfloss steak

blowy kite cake

gold show boat

high music terrace

tasty sun bunting

jellied sea guitar

new crash symphony

loud sand cats

tingling transistor bucket

blue happening theatre
jellied music dogs
green pier diva
mellow roundabout symphony
new sun poetry
hopping eels show
gold sport cats
high steak scene
cool transistor terrace
huge kite orchestra
blowy spring birds
red dance cloud
tasty boat cake
gay crash pavilion
loud sand bunting
lazy bucket art
happy guitar fish
tingling candyfloss sea

Edwin Morgan

Macaroni

Macaronic Poems
Numbers
Definitions
Rules
Conceptual Poems

Edict from Eden

eternal punishment
for grammatical error
– instead of a sentence,
a sin tax.

David Hopkins

Feast before Babel

kald komkommer suupu

andor

spielpastete

andor

allspezie id condemented worsts

rotituktuk

andor

bifftrosti

mith misturati grins

priklplommi

andor

allcoocook

andor

panefteret

andor

yseklijl

andor

waltbeere bloom mith briefbrot

kaff mith edesötsies

Alastair Fowler

Sonetto

sopra la Morte Di Antonio Dargasso philosopho, platonico, philologo,
phisiognomo, astrologo et theologo, Monacho Dominicano. A la
Macoronesca. Obiit Lond. 10 May 1605.

Doncq is it vray que Atrapos te rapuit
tam subito, et non hablando meco?
O Cruda morte et com' amore ceco [?]!
Creca [?] cur corpus curis ita tabuit?
Dedans the Gipsier of his Ceruell habuit
of Scyence plus then any learned greço,
et cum de Mie lodi erat praeco
appresso Todos hombres, tunc euanuit.

Quid faciam in questo strano caso?
Cauar gli occhi and lacerat my petto,
romper my collo and tagliar this naso.
Guarda mi dios! non feray, for sospetto:
Yet shal I macerat my self in tali sorte
that his externe shal be my Inword morte.
prosopopoeia defunti
Non redamas, sed me vis In amore mori.

William Fowler (1560–1612)

Counting

Ounce	Instant	Archery
Dice	Distant	Butchery
Trice	Tryst	Treachery
Quartz	Catalyst	Taproom
Quince	Quest	Tomb
Sago	Sycamore	Sermon
Serpent	Sophomore	Cinnamon
Oxygen	Oculist	Apron
Nitrogen	Novelist	Nunnery
Denim	Dentist	Density

One to Twenty

Yan, tan, tethera, methera, pimp.
Sethera, lethera, levers, dovers, dick.
Yanadick, tanadick, tetheradick, metheradick, bumfit.
Yanabumfit, tanabumfit, tetherabumfit, metherabumfit, gigot.

from Change: a set of 64 playing cards

To play the game of CHANGE is to be in search of rules.

Rules, if formulated, are liable to change in unforeseen ways.

The game of CHANGE *represents one long admonition to careful scrutiny of one's own character, attitude and motives.*

Chance in all elements is a major factor in the game and should be used when dealing or selecting cards.

Play CHANGE alone, in groups, card by card, in suits, cooperatively, competitively, on the telephone, by post, however suits you.

The game may be played for a predetermined time span – by the minute, by the hour, by the week – but CHANGE is continuous.

Recognition is part of the process of CHANGE.

Enactment is part of the process of CHANGE.

Notice especially the moment of transition, the CHANGE from one card to another.

If you always have the same cards it is significant.

If you always have different cards that is significant.

CHANGE should not be confused with individual changes.

This is the game of CHANGE.

Play in the game of CHANGE can never by exactly the same twice.

Gerry Loose

tea top: a musical, spinning samovar.

the Tea Theatre: the highest theatre in the world; home of the Darjeeling Drama,

tea hod: small hod for carrying tea bricks in Tibet.

tea square: an impotent Dervish.

tea cloud: a high calm soft warm light gold cloud, sometimes seen at sunset.

teafish: bred by the Japanese in special fish-farms, where it feeds on tannin-impregnated potato extract, this famous fish is the source of our 'instant fish teas', tasting equally of fish, chips, and tea.

tea cat: species of giant toad found in South India; it is not a cat, and has no connection with tea.

grey tea: used of a disappointment. E.g. 'Harriet got her grey tea that night.'

brown bolus tea: an old-fashioned medicine, of which the true recipe has been lost.

tea stays: so called, in Edwardian times, because they added elegance to the gestures of a hostess pouring tea.

sea tea: sailors' term for plankton bouillon.

Edwin Morgan

Four Conceptual Poems

1.

How – if at all – would Plato have amended *The Republic*, given a present-day awareness of the tensile strength of alloys?

Illustrate with specific examples.

2.

'Fuck "restricted register" – for starters look at the eyebrows' (Tom Leonard). In what ways do extra-verbal kinetics affect class-accent communication?

Punctuate your answer accordingly.

3.

'In any observer-observed evaluative situation, it is vital that qualitative judgment does not become a form of theft: the theft, from the observed, of the ability to evaluate a larger context which would include the observer amongst the components to be evaluated.'

How do you see yourself in relation to *this* poem – as observer or observed? Make your answer diagrammatical.

4.

'The popularity in Scotland of the line, "A man's a man for a' that", is enhanced by the fact that so many Scottish men are uncertain of their sexuality.'

Assess the role of the counter-dependent personality in Scottish Literature. You may refer to the role of the dependent personality in Irish Literature, if you wish.

Tom Leonard

from A Life Exam

1. Rewrite *The Waste Land* using only
   English words of one syllable.

2. Rearrange the entire Bible
   into two columns, one headed
   KNOWLEDGE, the other WISDOM.

24. With a view to bioengineering
    suggest at least six names for new animals.

31. How many words can be made from letters of the Western
    alphabets?

58. Summarize in 10 words the history of your greatest love.

61. Could you tell by the syllabic patterns
    of names of people you met how much
    they would come to mean in your life?

69. Write here the names of those you pray for.

Robert Crawford

A Horse's Meal

Children's Poems

Herdboys' Flyting

Buckalee, buckalo,
Buckabonnie, buckabo,
A fine bait amang the corn,
What for no?

A lippie or a peck,
A firlot or a bow,
Sorrow brak the herd's neck
Ower a foggie knowe.

*

Zeenty, peenty, heathery, mithery,
Bumfy leery over Dover;
Saw the King o Heazle Peasil
Jumpin ower Jerus'lem Dyke;
Black fish, white troot,
Eerie, oorie, you're oot.

*

Onica bonica
Susie borica
Onica bonica out.

Sweetie Rhyme

Ane's nane,
Twa's some,
Three's a pickle,
Fower's a pun,
Five's a denty,
Six is plenty,
Seeven's a horse's meal.

*

Broo, broo, brenty,
Ee, ee, winkie,
Nase, nase, nebbie,
Cheek, cheek, cherry,
Mou, mou, merry,
Chin, chin, chackie,
Catch a flee, catch a flee!

*

Collop Monday,
Pancake Tuesday,
Ash Wednesday,
Bloody Thursday,
Lang Friday,
Hey for Saturday efternin;
Hey for Sunday
At twal o'clock,
Whan a the plum puddins
Jump oot o the pot.

Skipping Rhyme

Teddy bear, teddy bear, turn around,
Teddy bear, teddy bear, touch the ground,
Teddy bear, teddy bear, one two three,
Teddy bear, teddy bear, count the sheep with me.

A, B, C, D, etc.
(When the person skipping trips, they have to give a name beginning with that letter.)

Cottage, mansion, flat,
Cottage, mansion, flat, etc.
(When the person skipping trips, that's where they'll live.)

1, 2, 3, 4, etc.
(When the person skipping trips, that's how many children they'll have.)

A, B, C, D, etc.
(When the person skipping trips, they have to give all their children names beginning with that letter.)

Commentaries

Detached Sentences on Concrete Poetry

Concrete poetry is not a visual but a silent poetry.

Concrete poetry was considered childish because it was seen and not heard.

The Muse of concrete poetry reversed Mnemosyne's gift; depriving the poet of song, she gave him sweet eyesight.

Ian Hamilton Finlay

Chrestomathy

Alphabets, like musical scales, or fingers and toes, or stars and constellations, or stone circles, or abacuses, or sea waves, or comets and eclipses, or genealogies, or bird and fish migrations, owe their interest and appeal to a combination of regularity and chance. Both the traditional unifying factor of a repeated formula and the underlying sense of huge permutations are present in such a manner as to suggest that power, and not merely play, is a concern of alphabets. Creative power can be expected to manifest itself from the combinative developments and experiments of 20 or 30 letters, yet there is also, and it can still be felt, a ritualistic power in the alphabet, very ancient, transmitted to children, used by poets and composers and advertising-men, found too in supposedly rational transformations in libraries, in hospitals, in stadiums, in astronomy, in war, in industry. Depending on the purposes for which letters in sequence are employed, a surprising range of human experience seems to be willing or anxious to cling to this fish-ladder. Early poetry – whether oral secular ballads or religious psalms and hymns – might well have thought of alphabetic stanzas as a mnemonic aid, as it might think of formulaic devices, or parallel clauses, or rhyme; but in the end something more than this is involved, where for example the alphabetic Hebrew Psalms, when properly translated, convey to us a sense of diligently covering all aspects of their theme ('from A to Z' as the cliché says) and by their ingenuity (if this is not forced) returning talents to God. For in many things that might appear to our sensibilities to be merely mechanical or merely playful, there is an unsuspected soul of seriousness, and no one who has read the dark, tortured Latin of the alphabetic *Altus* of St Columba, with its strong sense of transcendence and judgement, will fall back on the dismissive idea that medieval monks had too much time on their hands. Given the fact that games may be playful, mortal, didactic, or perhaps divine, there may be no unbridgeable distance between a Hebrew Psalm and a child's absey-book, or between a Lear animal alphabet and a crystallographic formula. However that may be, and whatever use one makes of it, the simple procession or progression of the alphabet has in itself a certain character: the landmarks of the most-employed letters like A, E, I, N, O, and T (known mentally but disguised by the dictionary where initially-favoured C, P, and S loom much larger), the quirky snags of J-K and Q, very native but under-used, the weird exotic W-X-Y-Z straggling finally like fragments to shore against your ruins (also, like the end of *The Waste Land*, full of foreign quotations). I am speaking, too, only of English; in a Hungarian dictionary the letter K is as fat in entries as in English it is thin, and P is as niggardly as with us it is prolific: each language must therefore carry its own feelings about the letters which compose it, even though it is also linked to other tongues by alphabetisation itself. Joyce beseeches us in his multi-languaged *Finnegans Wake* (pp.18-19): '(Stoop) if you are abcedminded, to this claybook, what curios of signs (please stoop), in this allephbed! Can you rede (since We and Thou had it out already) its world? It is the same told of all ... Olives, beets, kimmells, dollies, alfrids, beatties, cormacks and daltons.' Knowledge of Psalm 119 would remind us that the Hebrew 'allephbed' begins Aleph, Beth, Gimel, Daleth, which Joyce has shown to be part of a more universal 'allforabit'. Literature, by chance in the event as well as by design in the etymology, has also been called 'letters', and although the last 'man of letters' in the old professional sense was perhaps Edmund Wilson, new men of letters from Schwitters and the futurists to Cobbing and the concretists have emerged to remind us of the literation basis of languages and language culture. Much of this recent poetic material drives us back to an awareness of our alphabets which is both visual and oral. Neruda pleads in his 'Ode to Typography': 'Letters,/continue to fall/like precise rain/along my way', and likens letters also to waves, to flowers, to birds, to chessmen, to things both seen and heard, waiting to be brought 'to the unappealable/order/of intelligence'. Of course that order may be playful. Play effects readily arise when attention is drawn to rearrangeable components, especially if sound and sight are both involved. Qualities will appear, too, which may be hard to describe merely in terms of 'comedy' or 'seriousness', perhaps reminding us of the ambiguous nature of speech and language – instruments equally of communication and secrecy. Reading alphabet poems may serve to revive the suspect delights of incantation, on the one hand, or it may on the other hand suggest the nearness of poetry to code, which could cause as much uneasiness. Still, I am sure that many people will find Peter Mayer's volume a surprising and attractive collection, edging out their thoughts and reactions into some less-than-familiar areas and possibly whetting their appetites for further consideration of the mysteries inherent in the relations between sound and meaning, between graphic shape and sound, and between graphic space and meaning. There is much here that has yet to be explored. Use and wont can dull us to what we really speak and read. Verse alphabets, in being both very old and very new, may connect a good spark. We need at times to reconsider all the lost lines of development, or what might seem to have been lost lines of development, in order to make sure that the Psalmist, or Columba, or even Kurt Schwitters not so long ago, did not have his hand on some lever which still has access to power. Xeroxes of past effects are not what is wanted. 'Yonder' is only a penultimate. Zones of force are what such a volume offers, to be entered and felt; enter!

Edwin Morgan (Foreword to *A Chrestomathy*)

The Language of Today

We ought perhaps to conclude that the language of today must have certain things in common with poetry, and that they should sustain each other both in form and substance. In the course of daily life this relationship often passes unnoticed. Headlines, slogans, groups of sounds and letters give rise to forms which could be models for a new poetry, just waiting to be taken up for meaningful use. The aim of the new poetry is to give poetry an organic function in society again, and in doing to restate the position of the poet in society ... So the new poem is simple and can be perceived visually as a whole as well as in its parts. It becomes an object to be both seen and used: an object containing thought but made concrete through play-activity, its concern with brevity and conciseness ... Being an expert both in language and the rules of the game, the poet invents new formulations. By its exemplary use of the rules of the game the new poem can have an effect on ordinary language.

Eugen Gomringer, from 'From Line to Constellation', 1954 (trans. Mike Weaver)

Letter to Pierre Garnier

I feel that the main use of theory may well be that of concentrating the attention in a certain area – of providing a context which is favourable to the actual work. I like G. Vantongerloo's remark: 'Things must be approached through sensitivity rather than understanding ...'; this being especially acceptable from Vantongerloo since he is far from being against understanding (it seems to me) – his 'must' I take to mean 'must' because the world is such and we are so ... An understanding (theoretical explanation) of concrete (in general) poetry is, for me, an attempt to find a non-concrete prose parallel to, or secular expression of, the kind of feeling, or even more basically, 'being,' which says, if one listens carefully to the time, and if one is not sequestered in society, that such-and-such a mode of using words – this kind of syntax, this sort of construction – is 'honest' and 'true' ...

One of the Cubists – I forget who – said that it was after all difficult for *them* to make cubism because they did not have, as we have, the example of cubism to help them. I wonder if we are not all a little in the dark, still as to the real significance of 'concrete' ... For myself I cannot derive from the poems I have written any 'method' which can be applied to the writing of the next poem; it comes back, after each poem, to a level of 'being,' to an almost physical intuition of the time, or of a form ... to which I try, with huge uncertainty, to be 'true.' Just so, 'concrete' began for me with the extraordinary (since wholly unexpected) sense that the syntax I had been using, *the movement* of language in me, at a physical level, was no longer there – so it had to be replaced with something else, with a syntax and movement that would be true of the new feeling (which existed in only the vaguest way, since I had, then, no form for it ...). So that I see the theory as a very essential (because we are people, and people think, or should think, or should *try* to think) part of our life and art; and yet I also feel that it is a construction, very haphazard, uncertain, and by no means as yet to be taken as definitive. And indeed, when people come together, for whatever purpose, the good is often a by-product ... it comes as the unexpected thing. For myself, on the question of 'naming,' I call my poems 'fauve' or 'suprematist,' this to indicate their relation to 'reality' ... (and you see, one of the difficulties of theory for me is that I find myself using a word like 'reality' while knowing that if I was asked, "What do you mean by reality?," I would simply answer, "I don't know ...."). I approve of Malevich's statement, 'Man distinguished himself as a thinking being and removed himself from the perfection of God's creation. Having left the non-thinking state, he strives by means of his perfected objects, to be again embodied in the perfection of absolute, non-thinking life ...' That is, this seems to me, to describe, approximately, my own need to make poems ... though I don't know what is meant by 'God.' And it also raises the question that, though the objects might 'make it', possibly, into a state of perfection, the poet and painter will not. I think that any pilot-plan should distinguish, in its optimism, between what man can construct and what he actually is. I mean, new thought does not make a new man; in any photograph of an aircrash one can see how terribly far man stretches – from angel to animal; and one does not want a *glittering* perfection which forgets that the world is, after all, also to be made by man into his *home*. I should say – however hard I would find it to justify this in theory – that 'concrete' by its very limitations offers a tangible image of goodness and sanity; it is very far from the now-fashionable poetry of anguish and self ... It is a model, of order, even if set in a space which is full of doubt. (Whereas non-concrete might be said to be set in society, rather than space, and its 'satire,' its 'revolt,' are only disguised symptoms of social dishonesty. This, I realise, goes too far; I do not mean to say that society is 'bad.') ... I would like, if I could, to bring into this, somewhere the unfashionable notion of 'Beauty,' which I find compelling and immediate, however theoretically inadequate. I mean this in the simplest way – that if I was asked, "Why do you like concrete poetry?" I could truthfully answer "Because it is beautiful."

Ian Hamilton Finlay, from a letter to Pierre Garnier, September 17th 1963

Concrete poetry

I became interested in concrete poetry as a means of producing economically and arrestingly certain effects which would not otherwise be possible. These effects I still consider to be within the realm of poetry, though the use made of graphic space, and the exaggeration of such visual or sonic gestalts as exist in embryo in all poems, are clearly beginning to draw the poem over into other areas – painting, sculpture, advertising, music. In my own work I don't feel that the boundary into these other areas is crossed, because I have a strong sense of solidarity with words as part of a semantically charged flux, and in so far as I isolate or distort them I do this in obedience to imaginative commands which come through the medium of language and are not disruptive of it. This means that each of my poems has a 'point' and is not just an object of contemplation, though it is also that. I like to hear the semantic mainsheets whip and crack, but not snap. I like to extend the possibilities of humour, wit and satire through concrete techniques and although this involves 'play', whether of words, letters or punctuation, it must be an imaginative and therefore fundamentally serious kind of play.

I have always been interested in the plastic arts as well as in poetry. I don't find difficulty in accepting visual as well as aural impacts as legitimate targets for a poet. In all poetry which is written down or printed, a part of the effect is bound to be visual. Line-length, open or close texture, long or short words, light or heavy punctuation, use of capitals, exclamation marks, rhyme – all these produce characteristic variations of effect and induce different reactions in the viewer even before the viewer becomes in the strict sense a reader. A page of Milton's blank verse with its bristling and serried paragraphs looks quite different from a page of Wordsworth's, clear, open, light, loose, untormented. The phrasal dashes in Allen Ginsberg's long free verse lines are like white horses breaking the powerful under-swell of a poetry of big movement. The delicate cat-paw placing of words in poems by William Carlos Williams, Zukofsky, Creeley, and Ronald Johnson is halfway between being a guide to the ear and a pleasure to the eye. A more committedly visual poetry like concrete is only emphasising and developing an already existing visual component of aesthetic effect. Concrete poems are therefore not in opposition to the spirit of poetry unless we demand that poetry should be able to be read aloud, or unless they move so far into the purely graphic or the mathematical that they are no longer making their appeal through language as such. Abstract painting can often satisfy, but 'abstract poetry' can only exist in inverted commas. In poetry you get the oyster as well as the pearl, and the pursuit of purity is self-defeating. The best visual or concrete poems, as it seems to me, acknowledge this fact inversely; their anatomy may be rigid and exoskeletal, but there is something living and provocative inside.

Edwin Morgan, from *Nothing Not Giving Messages*

Typewriter Art

The international concrete poetry movement of the 1950s and 1960s gave a new impetus to typewriter experiment, and also added a new element to it: semantic content. Poems combining the verbal with the visual were composed on the typewriter in increasing numbers. Some of these concrete poems could be realised in print or – later, when it was invented – with transfer lettering such as Letraset. But others, because of the difference between typesetting and typing, are difficult, or impossible, to realise in print. For instance, to superimpose one line on another in printing requires two separate lines of type to be set, two separate formes to be composed, and finally two separate printings – a costly operation. With the typewriter one simply pushes the carriage back to the beginning of the line, or uses the back-spacer, and starts typing again.

Another distinction between printing and typewriting is that print letters vary in width, an m or a w being much wider than an l, whereas the typewriter's characters are all the same width. This means that a typed text in which successive lines are reduced in length by one letter will have a straight diagonal outline. In print, the diagonal outline would come out irregular and the crisp geometry of the design would be lost. Several concrete poets have suffered from misguided attempts to translate their typewriter works into normal print (though a few printers do have a special 'typewriter' typeface with the letters all the same width) . . .

One traditional craft has a similarity to typewriter work: embroidery on canvas. This has a rectilinear grid on which the design is built up one stitch at a time. And where the embroiderer uses different coloured thread to produce light and shade and shape, the typewriter artist as a rule does so by choosing letters of varying densities.

Alan Riddell, from the introduction to *Typewriter Art*, 1975

100 Differences Between Poetry and Prose

poetry stops before the end of the margin
you can talk about prose without mentioning school
you don't read poetry to get from Glasgow to Saltcoats without noticing

John Menzies doesn't stock poetry
whoever heard of war & peace having the line as a unit of semantic yield
you can call a poem what you want and says it's poetic licence

poetry is the subliminal history of linguistic shape
ahem
poetry has four wheels, two wings and a pair of false teeth

poetry is the heart and the brain divided by the lungs
poetry is the world's oldest cock and fanny story

you don't get prose in anapaestic dimeters
nobody publishes their first slim volume of prose
aristotle never wrote The Proses

if you dribble past five defenders, it isn't called sheer prose
poets are the unacknowledged thingwaybobs

poetry is quintessentially contrapuntal
the square root of poetry is an ever-evolving quark
whenever Vergil looked in the mirror, he beheld an epic Latin poet

poetry is all the juicy bits in the juiciest order
poetry is jellied religion
pascal: if your labourers complain too much, try taking them to a poetry
    reading

prose goes scchhpludd
prose goes scchhpludd scchhpludd clomp clomp clomp
are you sitting comfortably

then I'll end

Tom Leonard

Notes

p.34 These are all the names of plastic model kit manufacturers.

p.40 from *Songs of the Press and other poems relative to the art of printing* Greenock 1833

p.44 This poem prefaced 'Ane Metaphoricall Invention of a Tragedie called Phoenix', in *The Essayes of a Prentise* (1584).

p.46 The Greek text, derived from a panegyric to Zeus in Book IV of *The Odyssey*, reads: 'Makaron to trin trismakarotate' – 'O thrice most blessed of the blessed of old.' 'Makaros' meaning the 'blessed' or 'heroic dead' also puns on the Scots word 'makar', poet.

p.50 'Rehab VI: Decus et tutamen: the legend on the English pound coin, meaning comely and protective, was the description of a coat of mail Aeneas awarded a boatman in *The Aeneid*. The ancient Harappan inscription, transcription and translation are quoted from an article in the *Scientific American*. Thunderstone: stone arrowheads, from even earlier times, were later thought to be the residue of thunderbolts.' (Peter McCarey)

p.51 *Passacaglia on DSCH*: premiered in 1963, this has been described as 'possibly the longest continuous movement in piano literature, with a playing time of around eighty minutes'. Stevenson has stated that '[one] passage was inspired by the idea of the Soviet hammer beating the Nazi swastika into a sickle ... as a contrast to that passage, but linked with it, is another in which I have combined the motif DSCH with the time-honoured motif BACH; as a symbol that Russian and German and the whole of mankind can and will live as brothers in harmony and peace'.

p.76-79 'From *The Empty Quarter* by Harry St. John Philby. The text for the book work *Empty Quarter* was reworked from the three chapters that chart Philby's two attempts, in 1932, to cross the Rub' al Khali desert, the true Empty Quarter of Arabia. The first attempt (the chapters entitled "The Veritable Desert" and "Retreat") was a near fatal disaster and the second ("The Waterless Waste") proved successful. For *Empty Quarter*

(1997, 140pp, A4) the three chapters were erased on the computer and only the beginning and end of each paragraph returned to the page in the form of a running map: the placement of the words reflecting their actual topographical alignment with the original text. In this abridged version three pages have been chosen randomly from that erased text. They have, however, been placed in their correct order of appearance in the book. (Jim Harold)

p.82 'The poem "Perfect" was first published, as printed here, in Hugh MacDiarmid's book, *The Islands of Scotland* (1939), but the words of the poem itself, except the first line, were written as prose by Glyn Jones in a short story, "Porth-y-Rhyd", published in a collection of his stories, *The Blue Bed* (London: Jonathan Cape, 1937). When this matter came to light in the correspondence columns of *The Times Literary Supplement* in January 1965 Hugh MacDiarmid claimed that "any plagiarism was certainly unconscious", but immediately made the "necessary explanations and apologies" to Glyn Jones, adding: "The poem will of course not appear again over my name." Through a misunderstanding, however, it was included, without comment, in MacDiarmid's *Complete Poems* (1978).' (From editors' notes in *Hugh MacDiarmid, Complete Poems*, Vol. I, Carcanet, 1994)

p.84-85 From a series of 'Constructivist Poems': 'Since the use of the term by the Constructivist painters was somewhat different, these might be labelled "texturalist poems", that is a reweaving of an existing text into another texture, previously only implicit. All the words and phrases, except for minor adjustments and connectives, are 'as given', then re-patterned.' (Gael Turnbull)

p.89 L. E. Kastner, editor of *The Poetical Works of William Drummond of Hawthornden* (Manchester University Press, 1913), noted: 'It is not unlikely that Drummond read about such puerilities as the 'pyramis', the 'fuzie', the 'lozenge', and the like, in the *Arte of English Poesie* attributed to Puttenham.'

p.90 First published in 1813; reprinted in *Radical Renfrew: Poetry from the French Revolution to the First World War*, edited by Tom Leonard, Polygon, 1990.

p.99 from 'Heraclitan Variations'; 'this text presents a paradoxical opposition between the old [Greek] name for the bow (biós), which in the unaccented form was indistinguishable from the ordinary word for life (bios) and the actual use of the instrument for hunting and warfare.' Charles M. Kahn, *The Art and Thought of Heraclitus*

pp.125-133 Finlay was invited to create a garden for the newly built Max Planck Institute, Stuttgart, named after the German physicist, Max Planck, in 1975. These designs mark the highpoint of the Concrete poetry phase of his work. This is the only complete garden he was to realise in this style.

The garden at Little Sparta, which Finlay created in collaboration with Sue Finlay, and, latterly, with Pia Simig, has been acclaimed as the most important work by a Scottish artist in modern times. The three 'poems' reproduced here are characteristic of the garden's poetic classicism. Each poem is sited within a composed area. The 'Fragile' stone is sited at the farthest edge of the garden, where it meets the moor. The inscription on the small island is taken from Hölderlin's poem 'Half of Life': 'With yellow pears/& filled/with Wild Roses/the Land/hangs down/into the lake.' The inscribed fishing boat names on the slate poem are taken directly from *Olsen's Fisherman's Nautical Almanack* as a homage to LN, the American poet Lorine Niedecker (1903–1970).

p.137 First published in 1853 in the *New Paisley Repository*; reprinted in *Radical Renfrew* (see previous note). 'The sentence that spirals from the centre of the top field "We canna want the rot" and its answer from the bottom field "It pays the rent" (the tit to the ewe) refers to articles in prior issues of the magazine which claimed that local farmers were able to make more money from compensation on their blighted potato-fields than from the sale of the potatoes if they remained healthy.' (Tom Leonard)

p.156-160 'Ninety separate three-word phrases for posters or postcards; these are all different, but are permutations and combinations of 18 adjectives and 36 nouns relating to a festive theme. They have been arranged here in five groups of 18 phrases, to help indicate how they have been randomised or rearranged as desired.' (Edwin Morgan)

Audio CD *The Syllabary* sets out every meaningful monosyllable of my language on a three-dimensional grid: initial consonant on the y-axis, vowel on the z, and terminal consonant on the x-axis. Some 2000 of a possible 5000 combinations contain words; some of those 'cells' contain one word, others as many as fifty (eg L*OO*SH contains only 'louche', while 'B*OO*Z' contains booze, bruise, blues, and several plural and verbal forms of other 'B*OO*' words).

The computer program presents each cell on screen, one at a time, and shifts in a random manner to the next syllable on the grid in either sense on any of the three axes. A sound file and a graphic file are to be associated with each cell, so it can work either as a screen saver or as a continuous but ever-changing narrative. Such is the framework.

In October 1997 I began to write a text for each of the cells; at the present rate of just over two per week, it will take a while to finish. Still, the textual labyrinth is already big enough to get lost in. The recording you will hear is a snapshot of part of one possible path through the syllabary. On the real thing, you never hear the same sequence twice ... (Peter McCarey)

Bibliography

Books

Abrioux, Yves, *Ian Hamilton Finlay, A Visual Primer*, Reaktion Books, London, 1985, 2nd edition 1992

Bann, Stephen, *Concrete Poetry: An International Anthology*, London Magazine Editions, 1967

Between Poetry and Painting, Institute of Contemporary Arts, London, 1965 (no editor given)

Finch, Peter, *Typewriter Poems*, Second Aeon/Something Else Press, 1972

Finlay, Alec, *Ian Hamilton Finlay, Chapman* magazine no. 78–79 (special issue), Edinburgh, 1994

Finlay, Alec, *Wood Notes Wild: Essays on the poetry and art of Ian Hamilton Finlay*, Polygon, Edinburgh, 1995

Glen, Duncan, *Akros* vol. 6 no. 18 (special Concrete Poetry issue), Preston, 1972

Higgins, Dick, *Pattern Poetry, Guide to an Unknown Literature*, University of New York Press, 1987

Mayer, Peter, *Alphabetical and Letter Poems: A Chrestomathy*, The Menard Press, London, 1978

Morgan, Edwin, *Collected Poems*, Carcanet, Manchester, 1990

Morgan, Edwin, *Collected Translations*, Carcanet, Manchester, 1996

Purser, John, *Scotland's Music*, BBC/Mainstream, 1992

Riddell, Alan, *Typewriter Art*, London Magazine Editions, 1975

Solt, Mary Ellen, *Concrete Poetry: A World View*, Indiana University Press, 1968

Williams, Emmett, *An Anthology of Concrete Poetry*, Something Else Press, New York, 1978

Articles

Barton, Edwin J., 'On the Ezra Pound/Marshall McLuhan Correspondence', at http://www.chass.utoronto.ca/mcluhan-studies/v1_iss1/1_1art11.htm

Glen, Duncan, 'The Unfathomable Ground of Scottish Poetry', in *Akros*, vol. 3 no. 7, March 1968

Miller, David, 'Magical Effects', in *London Magazine*, August/September 1977

Morgan, Edwin, 'Concrete Poetry', in *Peace News*, 20 August, 1965

Scobie, Stephen, 'Concrete Poetry in Retrospect', in *Cencrastus*, no. 22, 1986

Watson, Roderick, 'Hugh MacDiarmid and the Poetry of Fact', in *Stand*, vol. 9 no. 4, 1968

Zurbrugg, Nicholas, 'Treating the Text', in *Stereo Headphones*, summer 1974

Index of Authors

Bamforth, Iain — 60-61
Bellingham, David — 49, 138
Braga, Edgard — 111, 112
Brown, George Mackay — 47
Büchler, Pavel — 69
Clark, Thomas A. — 29, 148-49
Cockburn, Ken — 59, 147
Crawford, Robert — 171
Cuickshank, Helen B. — 95
Drummond, William — 89
Dunning, Colin — 108
Evans, Thomas — 144
Finlay, Alec — 74
Finlay, Ian Hamilton — 35, 39, 48, 83, 99, 106, 107, 115-119, 139, 142, 179, 183-185
Forrest-Thomson, Veronica — 152-53
Fowler, Alastair — 140, 164
Fowler, William — 165
Gillies, Valerie — 36
Glen, Duncan — 66-67
Goethe, Johann Wolfgang von — 83
Gomringer, Eugen — 110, 182-183
Gorman, Rody — 27, 98
Harold, Jim — 76-79
Henderson, Kevin — 32-33, 75, 141
Hopkins, David — 163
James VI — 44-45
Jandl, Ernst — 105
Johnson, Ronald — 120-121
Khlebnikov, Velimir — 104
Leonard, Tom — 25, 100, 170, 188-89
Loose, Gerry — 58, 68, 168
MacDiarmid, Hugh — 30, 82, 154
MacIndoe, George — 90
MacManus, Tony — 41

McCarey, Peter — 50, 102-03, 155
Meade, Gordon — 72-73
Morgan, Edwin — 31, 34, 43, 94, 104, 105, 109, 110, 111, 123, 124, 151, 156-60, 169, 179-182, 185-187
Morgan, Pete — 42
Murray, John — 57
Paterson, Don — 56
Rabelais, François — 62-65
Ransford, Tessa — 91
Reid, Alastair — 143, 166
Riddell, Alan — 92-93, 122, 187-188
Rimbaud, Arthur — 41
Rose, Dilys — 28
Stephen, Ian — 96-97
Stevenson, Ronald — 51
Turnbull, Gael — 55, 84-85
Urquhart, Donald — 80-81
Urquhart, Thomas — 62-65
Vicuña, Cecilia — 109
vries, herman de — 70-71
Whyte, Hamish — 150
Woods, Alan — 144
Young, Douglas — 46

Acknowledgements

Thanks are due to the following copyright holders for permission to reproduce the poems in this collection. While every effort has been made to trace and credit copyright holders, the Publishers will be glad to rectify any oversights in any future editions.

IAIN BAMFORTH: 'Unsystematic Anatomy' from *Open Workings* (© Carcanet, 1996). DAVID BELLINGHAM: 'homage to dom silvester houédard' (© David Bellingham/WAX366 1997). GEORGE MACKAY BROWN: 'Stella Cartwright (for her birthday – 15 May 1982)' from *For the Islands I Sing* (© John Murray). PAVEL BUCHLER: 'Carefree' from *Collected Poems*, (Morning Star Publications/Centre for Artist Books, © Pavel Buchler 2000). THOMAS A. CLARK: 'Coire Fhionn Lochan'; 'An Acre for George Crabbe'; 'An Acre for John Clare' (© Moschatel Press). KEN COCKBURN: 'Souvenirs' from *Souvenirs and Homelands*, (© Scottish Cultural Press, 1998). ROBERT CRAWFORD: 'A Life Exam' from *Spirit Machines*, (© Jonathan Cape, 1999) reprinted by permission of the Random House Group Ltd. HELEN B. CRUIKSHANK: 'Lily Lochs: Harris' from *Collected Poems* (© Reprographia 1971). COLIN DUNNING: 'Cluster', from *Contra Diction*, (Art.tm, 1998). THOMAS EVANS: 'Dehiscence' (© Thomas Evans, 2000). IAN HAMILTON FINLAY: 'Sound Poem Kit', from *A Pretty Kettle of Fish*, Wild Hawthorn Press (© WHP, 1974); 'Arcady (some questions on the poem)' (Tarasque Press 1968, © Ian Hamilton Finlay, 1968); *Some Things* (Longhouse, 1995, © Ian Hamilton Finlay 1995); 'Kennst Du' (© WHP, 1995); 'Heraclitean Variations', from *Heraclitean Variations* (© WHP, 1986); 'First Suprematist Standing Poem' (© WHP, 1965); 'Homage to Malevich', from *Rapel: 10 fauve and suprematist poems* (© WHP, 1964), 'Star/Steer' (Brighton Festival Publications, 1967, © Ian Hamilton Finlay, 1967); 'Sea-Poppy 1' (Tarasque Press 1966, © Ian Hamilton Finlay, 1966); 'Sea-Poppy 2' (© WHP, 1968); 'Ring of Waves' from *The Blue and Brown Poems*, Jargon Press (© Jargon Press 1968, © Ian Hamilton Finlay 1968); 'tendresse' from *Telegrams from my Windmill* (© WHP, 1964); 'Acrobats' (Tarasque Press, 1966, © Ian Hamilton Finlay 1966); 'Letter to Pierre Garnier', (*Concrete Poetry: A World View*, Indiana University Press, 1970, © Ian Hamilton Finlay, 1963). ALEC FINLAY: 'World Cup Team', from *World Cup/Cup du Monde* (© Morning Star Publications/Water Press/WAX366, 1998). VERONICA

FORREST-THOMSON: 'Variations from Sappho' from *Collected Poems and Translations*, (Allardyce, Barnett, © Jonathan Culler and the estate of Veronica Forrest-Thomson). ALASTAIR FOWLER: 'Safety Net for Practice Tower' from *Catacomb Suburb* (Edinburgh University Press, 1976 © Alastair Fowler, 1976). DUNCAN GLEN: 'Apple Blossoms, eastwards of Motherwell, 1806', from *21 Poems after Drawings etc.* (Akros © Duncan Glen, 2000). EUGEN GOMRINGER, extract from 'From Line to Constellation', 1954 (trans. Mike Weaver). RODY GORMAN: 'Ceileireadh (Earrann)', 'Do Gheas' from On the Underground (© Polygon, 2000). JIM HAROLD: 'Empty Quarter' (© Jim Harold, 1997). KEVIN HENDERSON: 'World Cup Team', from *World Cup/Cup du Monde* (Morning Star Publications/Water Press/WAX366, 1998). RONALD JOHNSON: 'Rook', 'Gorse', 'Raindrops', 'Thistle' (© estate of Ronald Johnson, 2001). TOM LEONARD: 'In the beginning was the word', 'Four Conceptual Poems', from *Intimate Voices 1965–1983* (© Galloping Dog Press, 1984); 'Nora's Place' from *Reports from Scotland*, (© Tom Leonard); extract from 'How I Became a Sound Poet' (Reports from the Present, Cape, 1995 © Tom Leonard). GERRY LOOSE: 'Change', (© Gerry Loose, Writers Forum). PETER MCCAREY: 'Rehab No. 6: (Shakespeare Sonnet LV)', 'Ring Tale' from *Town Shanties*, (© Broch Books, 1990); 'From the Sanskrit' from *In the Metaforest*, (© Vennel Press, 2000). HUGH MACDIARMID: 'On a Lone Shore', 'Perfect', extract from 'In the Slums of Glasgow' from *Hugh MacDiarmid: Complete Poems* (© Carcanet, 1994). TONY MCMANUS: 'Vools' from *Alchemie o the Word*, (Scots Glasnost, © Tony McManus, 1990). EDWIN MORGAN: 'The Chaffinch Map of Scotland', extract from 'The Dictionary of Tea', 'The Loch Ness Monster's Song', 'Pomander', 'Seven Headlines', 'Siesta of a Hungarian Snake', 'Unscrambling the Waves at Goonhilly' from *Edwin Morgan: Collected Poems* (© Carcanet, 1990); 'You were a good girl to me', 'From Deep to Deep', 'Ballad', 'Isle', 'Ha-oo! ha-oo! ha-oo!' from *Edwin Morgan: Collected Translations* (© Carcanet, 1996); 'Alpha' and 'Foreword to A Chrestomathy' from *A Chrestomathy* (© Menard Press, 1978); 'Festive Permutation Poem-happening for Brighton' (© Edwin Morgan, 1967); Cecilia Vicuña, translated into Scots by Edwin Morgan, from *Palabrar*mas/*Wurdwappin*schaw, (Morning Star Folio 5/2, 1994); 'Concrete Poetry', first printed in *Between Poetry and Painting*, ICA, 1965, reprinted in *Nothing Not Giving Messages*, ed. Hamish Whyte, (Polygon, 1990)

pocketbooks

Summer 1998

01   GREEN WATERS
     An anthology of boats and voyages, edited by Alec Finlay;
     featuring poetry, prose and visual art by Ian Stephen,
     Ian Hamilton Finlay, Graham Rich.
     ISBN 0 9527669 2 2; paperback, 96pp, reprinting.

Spring 2000

02   ATOMS OF DELIGHT
     An anthology of Scottish haiku and short poems, edited with an
     Introduction by Alec Finlay, and a Foreword by Kenneth White.
     ISBN 0 7486 6275 8; paperback, 208pp, £7.99.

03   LOVE FOR LOVE
     An anthology of love poems, edited by John Burnside and
     Alec Finlay, with an Introduction by John Burnside.
     ISBN 0 7486 6276 6; paperback, 200pp, £7.99.

04   WITHOUT DAY
     An anthology of proposals for a new Scottish Parliament, edited
     by Alec Finlay, with an Introduction by David Hopkins. *Without
     Day* includes an Aeolus CD by William Furlong.
     ISBN 0 7486 6277 4; paperback with CD, 184pp, £7.99 (including VAT).

Autumn 2000

05   WISH I WAS HERE
      An anthology representing the diversity of cultures, languages and
      dialects in contemporary Scotland, edited by Kevin MacNeil and
      Alec Finlay, with an Aeolus CD.
      ISBN 0 7486 6281 2 paperback, 208pp, £7.99 (including VAT)

06   WILD LIFE
      Walks in the Cairngorms. Recording fourteen seven-day walks
      made by Hamish Fulton between 1985 and 1999, *Wild Life*
      includes an interview with the artist by Gavin Morrison and an
      Aeolus CD.
      ISBN 0 7486 6282 0 paperback, 208pp, £7.99 (including VAT)

07   GRIP
      A new collection of darkly humorous drawings by David Shrigley,
      Grip is the largest collection of Shrigley's work published to date
      and includes 16 colour illustrations and an Afterword by Patricia
      Ellis.
      ISBN 0 7486 6238 9 paperback, 208pp, £7.99

Spring 2001

08   DISTANCE & PROXIMITY
      The first collection of Scottish poet Thomas A. Clark's prose
      poems, *Distance & Proximity* includes the ever-popular *In Praise
      of Walking*, as well as a number of previously unpublished works,
      accompanied by the suggestive textures of Olwen Shone's
      photographs.
      ISBN 0 7486 6288 X paperback, 128pp, £7.99

09   THE WAY TO COLD MOUNTAIN
      A Scottish mountains anthology weaving together poetry, nature
      writing and mountaineering adventures, edited by Alec Finlay,
      with photographs by David Paterson.
      ISBN 0 7486 6289 8 paperback, 208pp, £7.99

10   THE ORDER OF THINGS
      The Order of Things is an anthology of shape, pattern and concrete
      poems that explore the grain of language and imitate the forms of
      nature. It includes Renaissance pattern poems and contemporary
      concrete, sound and visual poetry. Edited by Ken Cockburn with
      Alec Finlay; with an accompanying CD.
      ISBN 0 7486 6290 1 paperback, 208pp, £7.99 (including VAT)

Autumn 2001

11   MACKEREL & CREAMOLA

A collection of Ian Stephen's linked short stories with recipe-poems, illustrated with children's drawings. *Mackerel & Creamola* draws on Stephen's deep knowledge of the Hebrides, sea lore, and his experiences as a sailor. With a Foreword by Gerry Cambridge and a CD featuring stories and a dash of harmonica.

ISBN 0 7486 6302 9 paperback, 208pp, £7.99 (including VAT)

12   THE LIBRARIES OF THOUGHT & IMAGINATION

An anthology of 'Bookshelves' selected by artists and writers, and an illustrated survey of artist projects celebrating books and libraries. Edited by Alec Finlay, with an Afterword edited by Olaf Nicolai featuring an anthology of imagined books.

ISBN 0 7486 6300 2 paperback, 208pp, £7.99

13   UNRAVELLING THE RIPPLE

Book Artist Helen Douglas' beautiful and striking portrait of the tideline on a Hebridean island. Published in full colour, *Unravelling the Ripple* unfolds as a single image that flows through the textures and rhythms of sand, sea-wrack, rock and wave, to reveal dynamic sensual and imaginative depths.

ISBN 0 7486 6303 7 paperback, 208pp, £7.99

Spring 2002

14   JUSTIFIED SINNERS
An archaeology of Scottish counter-culture (1960–2000), from Sigma and Conceptual Art to the Beltane Fire Festival and the K Foundation. Edited by Ross Birrell and Alec Finlay, illustrated throughout.
ISBN 0 7486 6308 8 paperback, 208pp, £7.99

15   FOOTBALL HAIKU
An anthology of 'Football Haiku' published to coincide with the 2002 World Cup in Japan and South Korea. Edited by Alec Finlay, with photographs by Guy Moreton and an audio CD.
ISBN 0 7486 6309 6 paperback, 208pp, £7.99 (including VAT)

Available through all good bookshops.

Book trade orders to:
Scottish Book Source, 137 Dundee Street, Edinburgh EH11 1BG.

Copies are also available from:
Morning Star Publications, Canongate Venture (5), New Street, Edinburgh EH8 8BH.

Website: www.pbks.co.uk

The Order of Things

An Aeolus CD

1. *Interview* – Edwin Morgan, performed by EM and Bob Cobbing.

2. *ma language is disgraceful* – Tom Leonard.

3. from *Unrelated Incidents* – Tom Leonard.

4. *Gagi beri bimba* – Hugo Ball, performed by David Hopkins.

5. from *The Syllabary* – Peter McCarey.

6. *Edwin Morgan Anagram* – Bob Cobbing.

7. *Canedolia: an off-concrete Scotch fantasia* – Edwin Morgan.

8. *The Day the Sea Spoke* – Edwin Morgan.

9. *Ceileireadh/Twittering* – Rody Gorman, air aithris le Sìm MacCoinnich agus air a chlàradh le Ciarán Folan, Sabhal Mòr Ostaig, An t-Eilean Sgitheanach (performed by Simon MacKenzie and recorded by Ciaran Folan, Sabhal Mor Ostaig, Isle of Skye).

10. *Blues and Peal: Concrete 1969* – Edwin Morgan.

11. *Sleep is Serious* – David Hopkins.